John Robertson

RUSSIA IN REVOLUTION

Oxford University Press

Oxford University Press, Walton Street, Oxford OX2 6DP

Oxford   New York   Toronto
Delhi   Bombay   Calcutta   Madras   Karachi
Kuala Lumpur   Singapore   Hong Kong   Tokyo
Nairobi   Dar es Salaam   Cape Town
Melbourne   Auckland

and associated companies in
Beirut   Berlin   Ibadan   Mexico City   Nicosia

Oxford is a trade mark of Oxford University Press

ISBN 0 19 913275 5   © Oxford University Press 1982

First published 1982
Reprinted 1984, 1985

Phototypeset by Tradespools Limited, Frome, Somerset
Printed and bound in Hong Kong

CONTENTS

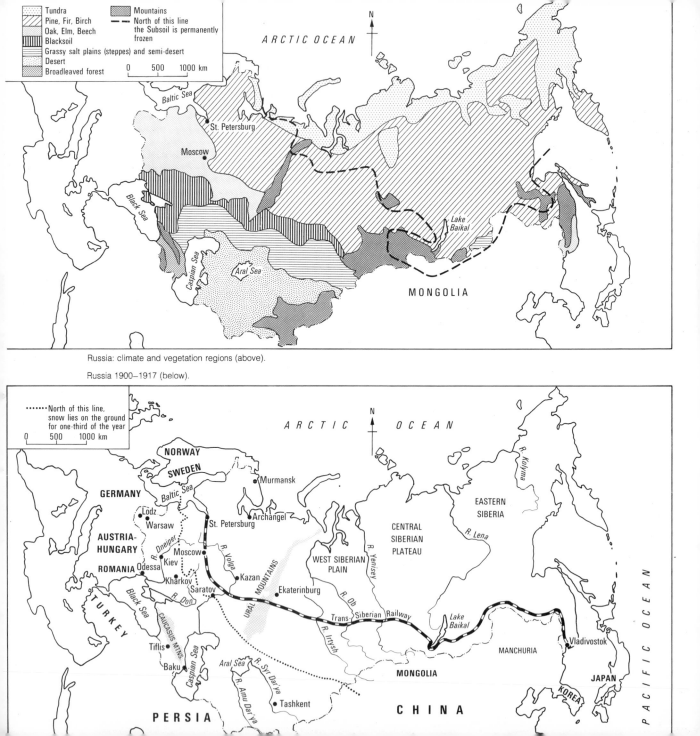

Key (top map):

- Tundra
- Pine, Fir, Birch
- Oak, Elm, Beech
- Blacksoil
- Grassy salt plains (steppes) and semi-desert
- Desert
- Broadleaved forest
- Mountains
- ― ― ― North of this line the Subsoil is permanently frozen

0   500   1000 km

ARCTIC OCEAN

N

Baltic Sea

St. Petersburg

Moscow

Black Sea

Caspian Sea

Aral Sea

Lake Baikal

MONGOLIA

Russia: climate and vegetation regions (above).

Russia 1900–1917 (below).

Key (bottom map):

······· North of this line, snow lies on the ground for one-third of the year

0   500   1000 km

N

ARCTIC OCEAN

NORWAY

SWEDEN

GERMANY

Murmansk

Lodz

Warsaw

Baltic Sea

St. Petersburg

Archangel

AUSTRIA-HUNGARY

R. Dnieper

Moscow

R. Volga

Kazan

R. Kolyma

EASTERN SIBERIA

CENTRAL SIBERIAN PLATEAU

R. Lena

ROMANIA

Odessa

Kiev

Kharkov

Saratov

Ekaterinburg

WEST SIBERIAN PLAIN

R. Yenisey

URAL MOUNTAINS

R. Ob

TURKEY

Black Sea

CAUCASUS MTNS

R. Don

Tiflis

Baku

Caspian Sea

Aral Sea

R. Irtysh

Trans-Siberian Railway

Lake Baikal

MANCHURIA

Vladivostok

JAPAN

KOREA

PACIFIC OCEAN

R. Syr Dar'ya

R. Amu Dar'ya

Tashkent

PERSIA

MONGOLIA

CHINA

Chapter One

Russia in 1900

The Land

The Russian Empire in 1900 covered almost 23 million square kilometres, a quarter of it in Europe, the rest in Asia. It amounted to approximately one-seventh of the land area of the planet. This vast territory includes some of the major climatic and vegetation regions of the world.

Moving from north to south the tundra of the Arctic regions with its permanently frozen subsoil gives way to great forests of fir, pine and birch. In European Russia, near Moscow, these turn into deep woods of oak, elm and beech. Little of this area is fit for cultivation. In central and southern European Russia the area of rich blacksoil provides the most fruitful land for farming. This, in turn, peters out in the great, grassy, salt plains or steppes which stretch from west of the Caspian Sea almost to the borders of Mongolia. Moving further south still the steppes fade into the arid deserts of central Asia. Little of the steppes and less of the desert is suitable for cultivation. Only the herding of sheep and camels are possible in the deserts of Turkmenia and Kazakhstan.

Approaching Russia from the west one encounters a vast plain stretching from Poland to western Siberia. This Eurasian Plain is broken only in Europe by the great navigable rivers, the Dneiper, the Don and the Volga and by the Ural mountains which effectively separate European Russia from its Asiatic hinterland. To the east of the Urals the West Siberian Plain reaches south to the Aral Sea and is cut by several huge rivers, the Ob, the Irtysh and the Yenisey which, though navigable, are ice-bound for six months of the year. The Eurasian Plain provides a basis for the growing of a great variety of cereal crops such as wheat, rye, barley, millet, and corn, as well as sugar beet, sunflowers and hemp.

The historian, W.H. Chamberlin, has written:

'Rich in some mineral resources and in forests, with a number of large navigable rivers, the Eurasian plain is subject to two natural disadvantages which unmistakably retarded Russia in its development. The severe winters and the short planting season lower the productivity of agriculture, while the land-locked character of the territory around Moscow, the centre from which the building up of the Russian state proceeded, seriously obstructed trade . . . with the outside world and contributed to the building up of a psychology of isolation.'

The People

In 1900 the population of the Russian Empire was around 128 million, most of whom were concentrated in the rich farming lands of the west and north-west. Most Russians were peasants living and working close to the land. There were few towns and cities of any great size and, with the exception of Tashkent, were all to be found in European Russia.

European Russia in 1900

Map legend:
- Pale of Settlement
- 0 300 600 km

Moscow at the end of the nineteenth century

Population of Russian Cities in 1897

City	Population
St. Petersburg	1,260,000
Moscow	1,040,000
Warsaw	680,000
Odessa	400,000
Lodz	310,000
Riga	280,000
Kiev	250,000
Kharkov	170,000
Tiflis	160,000
Tashkent	160,000
Vilna	150,000
Saratov	140,000

But only about half of the total population was made up of 'Great Russians'. Some 200 nationalities went to make up the Russian Empire of whom a quarter were non-Slav and perhaps a fifth were non-Christians. There were Roman Catholic Poles, Lutheran Finns and Estonians, some 5 million Jews, around 23 million Muslims among the numerous Tartars, Uzebeks, Kazakhs, Kurds and Turkmenians of central Asia, Buddhists and Pagans among the tribes of the Siberian Far East, and Byelorussians, Georgians and Ukrainians who, like the Russians followed the rites of the Orthodox Church.

The Russian Empire therefore was made up of a bewildering mixture of racial, linguistic and religious groups who varied enormously in levels of civilization, cultural traditions and ways of life. The central government tried to destroy the customs of the minorities by a process of 'russification'; forbidding the use of local languages in schools and attacking religious customs. These measures aroused resentment, and sometimes rebellion, in the subject peoples who wished to preserve their national characteristics. Such outbursts by the

Some of the many nationalities included in the Russian Empire:
1 Armenians
2 Caucasians (about to sacrifice goats and sheep to pagan gods)
3 Slavs
4 Boys from Bukhara in Uzbekistan
5 Tribal people from Western Russia (near Archangel)
6 The Karakalpak people of Turkmenistan

phylactery

Orthodox Jew at prayer

Assignment

1 Why is so little of Russia suitable for the growing of crops?
2 What 'natural disadvantages' kept back Russia's economic development?
3 Why were there frequent clashes between Russians and the members of minority races?
4 Why do you think Russia had few towns or cities of any size?
5 What factors made Russia difficult to govern?

The Government

Tsar Nicholas Russia in 1900 was ruled by Tsar Nicholas II, a member of the Romanov dynasty which had held the throne since 1613. His title was 'Emperor and Autocrat of all Russia'. Article One of the Fundamental Laws of the Empire 1892 stated that:

> 'The Emperor of all the Russias is an autocratic and unlimited monarch. God himself commands that his supreme power be obeyed, out of conscience as well as fear.'

Nicholas had been brought up to believe in the virtues of absolute power but he was totally lacking in the qualities necessary to wield it. Aged twenty-six, in 1894, when he succeeded his formidable father, Nicholas appeared 'charming, slight, boyish' but 'lacking all sense of purpose except to carry out the will of God as his obedient adjutant on earth'. His father had thought little of his abilities and had done nothing to educate him in the tasks of monarchy and the business of running the state. His father's sudden death in the Crimea threw Nicholas into panic and despair.

The Tsar had the right to nominate the ten members of his ministerial council whose function was to run the government. Each minister was

Poles were put down by military force, while the Jews were herded into certain provinces known as the _Pale of Settlement_.

Russia, because of her vast size, poor transport system, harsh climate, general backwardness and isolation and her great variety of peoples, was extremely difficult to govern. A problem made more acute by the position of the capital, St. Petersburg, built on the Gulf of Finland at the north-western extremity of the Empire. Here the Emperor or Tsar held his court and ruled Russia.

The young Nicholas and his wife, Alexandra

Nine-year old Alexis, heir to the throne, and a haemophiliac, is carried by a cossack at the Romanov Tercentenery celebrations.

individually responsible to the Tsar. There was no collective cabinet responsibility. Nicholas had the right to dismiss ministers at will but he seldom had the courage to do so to their face.

The Tsar also had the right to nominate the sixty members of the Council of State, whom he could consult regarding the introduction of certain laws. He preferred brainless, loyal mediocrities who would not threaten his authority. One member of the Council wrote despairingly of Nicholas's style of government: 'There is nothing consistent or firmly directed'.

Nicholas was a weak and indecisive man. He cared little for politics or public life and preferred to devote his time and interests to his family. He was totally unaware of the radical and often violent changes which were taking place within Russian society at this time. His response to problems he did not understand was to reassert his claims for absolute power – 'Know that I shall maintain the principles of autocracy just as firmly and unflinchingly as it was preserved by my unforgettable dead father' – and then use the army to crush any opposition which might arise. An American writer has concluded:

'Nicholas was obviously inadequate to the demands of his exalted position and this was an inadequacy for which no degree of charm, or courtesy, of delicacy of manner, could compensate.'

Tsaritsa Alexandra   In November 1894 Nicholas married Princess Alix of Hesse-Darmstadt. On her marriage she adopted the Russian name of Alexandra Feodorovna and, with all the fervour of a convert, entered the Orthodox Church. She was to become the dominant influence in Nicholas's life and a staunch upholder of autocracy.

Alexandra was a devoted wife and mother. In November 1895 she gave birth to the first of four daughters – Olga, Tatiana, Marie and Anastasia – and, in 1904 to a son, Alexis. Their joy, in the birth of an heir to the throne, was short-lived when it was discovered that the Tsarevich had haemophilia. This disease of the blood, which was found in the male line of the House of Hesse, was transmitted to Alexis through his mother. The slightest knock or bruise can cause internal bleeding and, as the blood refuses to clot, it frequently causes swellings accompanied by intense pain in the joints.

The illness of the Tsarevich increased the tendency of the Royal Family to shut themselves off from the outside world inside their apartment in the Alexander Palace at Tsarskoye Selo. The guilt felt by the Tsaritsa regarding her son's illness, and the inability of the doctors either to cure the disease or even to ease the boy's pain, strengthened those qualities of religious fervour and mysticism which Alexandra already possessed to a high degree. It also made her the prey of a number of bogus holy men and faith healers of whom the most successful was an uncouth, dissolute peasant from Siberia, Gregory Rasputin.

The Bureaucracy The modern Russian bureaucracy or civil service was created by Speransky the chief minister of Alexander I between 1809 and 1811. Under successive Tsars it had grown steadily in size and influence and was graded into fourteen different ranks. By 1900 the system was heavily over-centralized and generated an excessive amount of paperwork. The higher ranks of the civil service had, over the years, included many brilliant conscientious men who had done much to modernize Russia but it had also contained many extreme reactionaries and men of doubtful character. Laziness and corruption were found at all levels; even many of the highest officials took bribes and stole enormous sums from public funds. For the small official, who was overworked and miserably underpaid, bribery was normal practice.

The Okhrana Those Russians who opposed the Tsar and his government were liable to attract the attention of the State Police Department, in particular its secret section usually known as the *Okhrana*. 'Like a gigantic spider this institution spread its web all over the country'. Anyone might arouse the curiosity of the Police Director and his undercover agents. Members of the Cabinet and even the Tsar's mother were under police supervision and had their mail intercepted.

Undercover agents were everywhere. Some made their way into the secret revolutionary societies, sometimes even organized them, and took part in political acts of violence. Indeed two Ministers of the Interior, Plehve and Stolypin, who were nominally in charge of the Police, were assassinated by undercover agents of the *Okhrana* posing as revolutionaries.

The Orthodox Church After 1721, the Orthodox Church had been turned into a government department called the Holy Synod, and was run by a lay official appointed by the Tsar, called the Chief Procurator. The priesthood however had considerable influence over the devout Russian masses and politically this was expressed in favour of the Tsar and autocracy, of Greater Russian nationalism and in hostility towards members of other churches or racial groups. The Church played a leading part in the russification campaigns waged by the Government against the Poles and the Jews.

A parish priest: with his family (left) and handing out bread to his parishioners (right)

The parish priest, in the words of one historian:

'was hardly, if at all better than the peasants around him. Not, as a rule, paid a salary by the State, he depended for his living on whatever his parishioners agreed to pay him, after some haggling, for weddings, funerals and christenings . . . The upper and middle classes looked down on him because of his inferior status, his poverty, his low educational standard . . . the intelligentsia . . . treated him with contempt and saw in him nothing but a government agent and a hypocritical tool of the possessing classes; the peasants, so often at loggerheads with him over church dues, suspected him of being mean and grasping . . .'

Assignment

1 What is an autocrat?
2 In what ways was Nicholas ill prepared to become Tsar?
3 Why do you think Alexandra became a victim of numerous faith healers and 'holy men'?
4 Outline the activities of the Tsarist secret police.
5 Why do you think many inhabitants of the Russian Empire were hostile to the Orthodox Church?

Chapter Two

The social classes

The Nobility

At the beginning of the reign of Nicholas II there were about 1.8 million members of the nobility in Russia, of whom two-thirds possessed hereditary titles. Not all of these were land-owners or even particularly wealthy. Titles of nobility were granted to men who achieved certain ranks in the armed forces or the civil service, or to professional men who received certain decorations for their services to the crown. Lenin, for example, was born a 'noble' for his father had achieved the rank of Chief School Inspector and received the order of St. Vladimir which permitted him an hereditary title. Some nobles were indistinguishable from the peasants alongside whom they ploughed, sowed and harvested. The Tartar nobles of Lithuania kept small farms and worked as tanners or as restaurant waiters.

A few great families enjoyed the social standing and esteem which is associated with a European aristocracy – though they were unlikely to be as wealthy. The ostentatious display associated with Russian nobility usually indicated great debts rather than great riches. The lesser gentry often had employment in the city and kept a family estate which they occasionally visited. Others took an active part in the running of their estates, and were largely responsible for any farming improvements that ever took place in Russia. This group was also responsible for much of the culture and civilization of nineteenth-century Russia. Tolstoy, Turgenev and Dostoevsky, Tchaikovsky and Glinka all sprang from the lesser gentry.

They enjoyed certain privileges. The office of Land Captain, responsible for supervising the peasant commune, was reserved for the gentry as were

Countess Carlow takes tea with her English governess and nannies

Army officers: many of whom were drawn from the nobility

Peasant Allotments At the Emancipation the peasants lost a large proportion of the land that they had formerly farmed as serfs; 25 per cent on average, but in some provinces more than 40 per cent. Most of the good land was retained by the gentry. At the same time the peasants lost their customary rights to cut timber and hay from the landlords' forests and meadows, and were no longer permitted to graze their cattle on common pasture. A Peasants Bank was set up in 1883 to help the peasants borrow money to buy or lease more land, but although this brought additional acreage into peasant hands it didn't decrease resentment, for the peasant believed that the land should belong to those who worked it.

Almsgiving, 1900

certain other local government functions. Certain schools were reserved for the children of the higher grades of nobility, as were commissions in the more fashionable regiments.

The Peasantry

Russia was largely a country of peasants. In 1914 some 85 per cent of the population lived in the countryside, and most of these earned their living from agriculture – 'Completely cut off from the general business and cultural trends of the world'. Until 1861, when they were freed by Alexander II, the Russian peasants had been serfs, owned by a land-owner and obliged to work three days per week on his land. In return, they received a plot of land for the family for which they paid in rents and services. While the Emancipation Acts of 1861 granted the serfs their freedom, they did not create conditions in which the peasant farmers could support themselves.

Redemption Payments The peasants were not given the land on Emancipation but were obliged to pay a form of compensation to their former owners. Since most of the peasants could not afford this, the government bought the land from the nobles then resold it to the peasants at 6 per cent interest over forty-nine years. The figure set for repayment was too high and the method of calculation penalized the peasant with a small plot. Repayments were constantly in arrears and redemption dues were eventually abolished in 1907. Until that time, however, they helped to keep the peasants poor and provided a continuing source of discontent.

The Village Commune Although the peasants gained personal freedom by Emancipation much of this new-found liberty was lost to the village commune or *Mir*. This institution isolated the peasants from the rest of the population and subjected them to special laws administered, after 1889, by Land Captains chosen from the gentry. The *Mir* had existed in many areas before 1861 but, because the government wished to deal with the peasants as a whole rather than individually, its

A meeting of the *Mir*

powers were reinforced and extended to other districts. The commune was given the land granted to the peasants after Emancipation, and was made responsible for the payment of redemption dues and taxes.

At regular intervals the commune redistributed the land in accordance with the nature of the soil and the numbers in each peasant household. This system of communal strip farming had many disadvantages:

1 It imposed a common crop rotation.
2 It hindered improvements in farming technique and more intensive methods of cultivation.
3 It discouraged the use of fertilizers and hastened the exhaustion of the soil.
4 It wasted time and effort cultivating a number of narrow strips scattered over a wide area.
5 It wasted valuable land with boundary furrows.
6 It resulted in conflicts and violence at redistribution time.

The Peasant Household The right to a share of the village land belonged not to an individual but to a peasant household headed by a house elder. He was responsible for the payment of taxes and redemption dues to the commune and had wide powers over the earnings and property of the other members of the household. Relations between different members of the household therefore became very strained and, on occasions, exploded into violence.

Taxation The Russian peasant laboured under an enormous financial burden. Until early in the century he had to pay a poll-tax as well as his redemption dues. His land was taxed at seven times the rate of that held by the gentry. On top of this the government steadily increased taxes on spirits, tobacco, matches, sugar and kerosene. The peasant was obliged to sell most of his produce for export, to earn foreign currency to service the government's foreign loans, thus further depressing a standard of living which was already the lowest in Europe. Many peasants found themselves unable to provide enough food to feed their families far less produce a surplus with which to pay these taxes and redemption payments.

Overpopulation The plight of many peasants grew worse as the population in the countryside increased. In European Russia alone the numbers increased thus:

1865 – 50 million
1900 – 86 million
1914 – 103 million

Whereas the number of peasants increased by 27.8 per cent between 1877 and 1905, the land area at their disposal grew by only 24.2 per cent. The average size of family allotments decreased during this period. The situation was only partly eased by the migration of peasants to Siberia and to the towns, and many peasant families were unable to make a living from the land at their disposal. A feeling of acute land hunger developed and rioting took place in those provinces where land was in short supply.

The problem was only partly one of land shortage. The backwardness of Russian farming methods, and the lack of machinery and fertilizers resulted in a low yield in crops, but the peasants believed that their poverty resulted from the smallness of their allotments. This, they believed, could easily be remedied by seizing the estates of the nobility.

The Life of the Peasant The Russian peasants were a class apart. They were uneducated, usually illiterate, ignorant and prejudiced, isolated and

A Russian village scene: two long lines of wooden houses face each other across an unmade road

backward. They believed in the Orthodox Church and the Tsar. He was their 'little father' and, like Nicholas himself, they believed in an almost mystical union between the throne and the peasant masses: 'The Tsar took the serfs away from the landlords, therefore the Tsar alone must be lord over all the peasants. . . .'

These 'dark people' lived in villages stretched out on either side of an unmade road. The cottages rarely had chimneys and in winter the walls were often lined with dung to keep in the warmth. Dung and straw were used as fuel when no timber was available. The cottages were damp and leaking; the floors were of earth for in cold weather the lambs, pigs and cows were brought indoors.

Water was scarce, soap almost unknown; but some villages were fortunate in possessing a communal bath house. Skin diseases were common and epidemics of diphtheria and typhus occurred regularly.

A considerable number of peasants added to their income by working at some form of cottage industry, in which the whole family took part, or contracted themselves out as seasonal labour to the increasing number of factories and mills.

Assignment

1 Outline the privileges enjoyed by the Russian nobility.
2 Why were many peasants poorer as a result of Emancipation?
3 What were the drawbacks of a system of communal strip farming?
4 Why did peasant allotments grow smaller?
5 Do you agree that 'the problem was only partly one of land shortage'? Give reasons for your answer.

The Middle Classes

Russia did not possess a unified middle class or bourgeoisie in the fashion of Britain or western Europe. There were three distinct groups who had little in common: the civil servants or bureaucrats; the merchants or businessmen; and the group referred to as the intelligentsia.

Each group possessed a different outlook towards society and towards the Tsar. As for the civil servants: 'the standards of the bureaucrats were still those derived from the service gentry: the state was placed before the individual, military values above civil values and the good opinion of [their] superior was preferred to the approval of public opinion'.

The businessmen came into prominence in the late nineteenth century and were mostly from peasant stock. As a rule they accepted the autocracy and were indifferent to political rights and liberties, being concerned mainly with their profits.

The intelligentsia was largely made up from the ranks of doctors, lawyers, and writers. This group tended to reject the autocracy and the existing order of Russian society and provided most of the political leadership of the early twentieth century. They were closely associated with the growth of the *zemstva*.

A group of merchants, 1905

The Zemstva The Zemstva Act of 1864 had granted a limited form of self-government to rural areas. The right to vote was extremely limited but a form of county council was set up, followed in 1870 by a Municipal Act which granted the same rights to the towns. The *zemstva* did much good work and by 1914 had grown into an important factor in the life of the nation, as one writer explains:

'With untiring energy and remarkable sense of duty they proceeded to build schools, hospitals, dispensaries and orphanages. They organized experimental farms and instructed the peasants in the best methods of handling their crops and livestock.'

Despite the suspicions of the peasantry and the hostility of the civil service the *zemstva* made great strides in bringing literacy and civilization to the Russian countryside. As another historian writes:

'Through their employment . . . of doctors, nurses, teachers, sanitary inspectors, engineers, economists and agronomists they gave

employment to a new class of reformers and radicals, intimately aware of peasant conditions and bitterly critical of what they saw.'

Industry and Workers

The Growth of Industry The extremely low standard of living of most of the Russian people had held back the growth of industry for many years, but with Emancipation came an increase in trade and with it a steady growth in the size of towns. However, it was not until 1890 that any rapid increase in industrial production took place. Much of the credit for this must go to Sergei Witte who held the posts of Minister of Transport and Minister of Finance from 1892 onwards.

Certain features marked out the growth of industry in Russia:
1 An emphasis on heavy industry, particularly railway construction (the Trans-Siberian Railway).
2 The concentration of industry in large units; by 1902 almost half the workforce was employed in

A Zemstva Council session

Russian industry in 1900

3 The Ukraine (coal, iron, metallurgy, chemicals)
4 Poland (textiles, coal, iron, chemicals)
5 The Urals (coal, iron, non-ferrous metals, metallurgy)
6 Baku (petroleum)
7 Transcaucasia (coal, manganese)

The Output of Russian Industry (millions of tons)

	1860	1900	1914
Coal	0.3	16.0	36.0
Pig Iron	0.3	2.7	4.8
Steel	0.002	2.5	4.0
Oil	0.2	10.4	9.0
Cotton	0.05	0.2	0.4

Industrial Workers By 1900 there were around 2¼ million industrial workers in Russia of whom around 50 per cent were the children of fathers who had themselves been factory workers. The growth in the numbers of industrial workers was due to peasants coming in from the countryside. Many of them retained their links with their native villages, keeping their strips of land to which they returned when unemployed, sick or old. Around 25 per cent of the workforce regarded industry as a part-time, largely winter, occupation spending the rest of the year working on the land. The St. Petersburg region had the highest proportion of permanent workers (90 per cent), most of whom worked in large enterprises.

factories with over 1,000 employees.
3 The great extent of government financial involvement; the state owned railways, factories and mines and lent huge sums to private business.
4 The dependence on foreign investment; vast sums were borrowed from France, Belgium and Germany to finance the growth of industry.

By the turn of the century there were seven main centres of industrial development inside Russia, with the biggest growth concentrated in the triangle formed by St. Petersburg – the Ukraine – Moscow. They were:
1 Moscow (textiles, metal processing, chemicals)
2 St. Petersburg (textiles, machine building, metallurgy)

Russian Industrial Workers 1900

Size of Individual Enterprises (employed hands)	Number of Enterprises	Total number of hands
from 1 – 10	2,366	17,314
from 11 – 100	11,900	432,430
from 101 – 500	2,717	616,594
over 500	894	1,253,139

The links between factory and village slowed down the process of industrialization and the formation of a permanent working class. This process was further hampered by the very low level of wages which made it impossible for the worker to support his wife and family without the help of his plot of land in his native village. Few workers could afford housing and lived in barracks provided by the employers. Some firms built barracks for only half their workers – the beds being occupied in shifts – while in others, married men and their families lived side by side with unmarried workers, in conditions which were severely overcrowded: 'with less than two cubic yards (1.5 cubic metres) of air space per man, and sometimes less than one cubic yard (0.7 cubic metres)'.

Conditions of Work The Russian worker was subject to unhealthy and insanitary working conditions and to a harsh factory discipline. The withdrawal of rent allowances and bonuses, the imposition of fines and the use of corporal punishment were all employed to keep the workers in line. Accidents were common and it was not until 1897 that a maximum working day of 11½ hours was

Foundry workers

Living conditions for the Putilov iron workers

established. A Factory Inspectorate was set up to enforce the laws relating to child labour and the employment of women, and did much good work despite the hostility of employers and the suppression of many of its reports by the government.

Trade Unions were illegal as were the strikes which rapidly became a feature of Russian industrial life. The strikes tended to be short-lived but were most common in the large enterprises. The government, which regarded 'the hiring of factory labour [as] not merely a civil contract but a matter of public interest irretrievably connected with public order and peace', moved police permanently into the factories (one policeman per 250 workers, one inspector per 3,000 workers) and frequently called on the Army to deal with strikers. This often led to bloodshed.

State Unions In an attempt to divert the genuine complaints of the workers, concerning wages and conditions, away from political activity and thus 'save' the workers from falling into the hands of the revolutionaries, the government decided to set up its own labour unions.

The policy was put into effect in 1901 by General Zubatov, head of the Moscow security police. He set up a Mutual Assistance League of Workers in the Mechanical Industry, which provided lecture courses and discussion groups designed to show the benefits of a non-revolutionary approach to social problems. Similar organizations were set up in other trades in different areas, but when in 1903 Zubatov unions led strikes in south Russia the employers put pressure on the government to have them disbanded. The industrial workers of Russia again found themselves outside society, with no alternative but to support those groups which called for the overthrow of autocracy.

Assignment

1 Outline briefly, in your own words, the views and attitudes of
   a) the bureaucrats
   b) the businessmen
   c) the intelligentsia
2 What type of work was carried on by the *zemstva*?
3 What were the main features of Russian industrial development?
4 For what reasons was Russia slow to create a full-time industrial working class?
5 Why did the government move police into the factories?
6 Explain the thinking behind the creation of the Zubatov unions.

Chapter Three

The opposition

The Liberals

Throughout nineteenth-century Russia there had existed groups of moderate minded people who disliked autocracy but could not bring themselves to support the extreme solutions of the revolutionaries. These Liberals consisted of members of the gentry, represented in the *zemstva*, teachers, doctors and vets employed by the *zemstva* and academics, lawyers and other members of the professional classes. They ranged in opinions from rather conservative *zemstva* leaders to radical intellectuals who could almost equally well be called socialists. Government hostility towards any united action by these people forced them into opposition.

In 1902 a journal called *Liberation* appeared, published in Germany and edited by a former Marxist, Peter Struve. He called for a united front of opposition groups ranging from revolutionaries to gentry liberals. This led to the setting up of an illegal party inside Russia known as the Union of Liberation. Its programme called for:
1 The abolition of autocracy and the establishment of a constitutional government.
2 Universal, secret, direct elections to be held in equal constituencies.
3 The right of self-determination for subject minorities, such as Poles and Finns.

In 1905 the Union of Liberation joined with a group called the Zemstvo Constitutionalists to form a new political party known as the Constitutional Democrats or Kadets.

Peasant Socialism

The failure of the autocracy to grant basic political rights or civil liberties, and the suppression of all dissent by the secret police, drove some members of Russian society to the belief that only by the complete overthrow of the Monarchy and all its agencies of repression could a better society be created inside Russia. They became revolutionaries.

Many of the early revolutionaries, such as Alexander Herzen and Peter Lavrov, believed that a uniquely Russian form of socialism could be established, based on the village commune. There would be no need to pass through the intermediate stages of middle class democracy and capitalism, such as existed in western Europe, and which many of the Russian revolutionary exiles found deeply distasteful.

Alexander Herzen, 1812–70

Peter Lavrov, 1823–1900

Lavrov believed that a revolution would only come about when the mass of the Russian people had become politically educated. This could only happen if the few educated members of society went out and spread democratic and socialist ideas among the illiterate peasantry. Herzen's slogan '*v narod*' – 'to the people' – was revived, and in 1873 and 1874 thousands of young students moved out into the factories and fields of Russia as doctors,

teachers, agricultural labourers and nurses, 'devoting themselves entirely to the poorest part of the population'. These *Narodniks* or Populists were to have a bitter awakening. As one writer puts it:

'They were jeered at, abused, sometimes beaten and stoned, reported to the police . . . Hundreds of these innocents were in fact arrested – over sixteen hundred between 1873 and 1877 – and sat in prison for years awaiting trial.'

Although most were acquitted they were later arrested by the secret police and sent off to exile in Siberia. The failure of the Populists forced the revolutionaries to adopt more extreme measures.

The Terrorist Tradition The belief that the state could be overthrown, by force exercised by well-disciplined, tightly-knit groups of revolutionaries was also part of the Russian tradition. Formulated first by the anarchist Michael Bakunin, and developed by younger revolutionaries such as Sergei Nechayev and Peter Tkachev, the idea of an

Revolutionaries in exile, Siberia 1895

Michael Bakunin, 1814–76

elite group, prepared to use terror tactics to seize power, gained support.

In 1876 there emerged from the ranks of the former Populists a well-organized secret opposition party called Land and Liberty. The writer, Kochan, describes this group:

'It demanded that the land be handed over to the peasants and that the State be destroyed . . . Here was a close-knit, disciplined, underground body, organized in regional groups with a membership of not much more than 200 with its own printing press and network of secret sympathizers . . .'

It lasted only until 1879 when its terrorist section, which had already assassinated leading government figures, split from the main body to form a group called People's Will. Its objective was the murder of Tsar Alexander II, which it achieved in March 1881.

But the assassination did not produce the expected uprising by the masses. For the time terrorism was discredited and the government moved swiftly to smash the revolutionary organizations, execute their leaders and consign the rank and file to prison or exile. There was an attempt to revive the terrorist movement in 1887 and a plot to assassinate Alexander III was uncovered. Five of the student conspirators, including Alexander Ulyanov, elder brother of the future Bolshevik leader, Lenin, were hanged.

The Socialist Revolutionaries The two strands of peasant socialism, combined with revolutionary terrorism, came together in 1901 with the formation of the Socialist Revolutionaries (S.R.s) under the leadership of Victor Chernov. The S.R.s did not have a coherent organization and membership of the party was never large or well organized. Chernov argued that a great peasant upheaval was inevitable, in which all land not held by the commune would be confiscated and distributed among the peasants according to need. In the meantime, it was necessary to unite as many opponents of the regime as possible with a programme which demanded basic political liberties, an 8-hour day in factory and village and a constituent assembly.

Agitation among the peasants was the main activity of the S.R.s but they also had a terrorist wing which conducted assassinations. This 'combat organization' whose membership was secret and independent of the rest of the party, was set up by

Victor Chernov, founder of the Socialist Revolutionaries

23

Gregory Gershuni. Its objectives were to disorganize the Tsarist State and to show the Russian people that a struggle against the forces of autocracy was already underway. It claimed two Ministers of the Interior, two Governors of Provinces and the Tsar's uncle among its notable victims. But the secret police had already penetrated the organization, for Yevno Azev had for many years played the double role of head of the Fighting Organization of the Socialist Revolutionary Party and agent of the Tsarist secret police, impartially betraying his comrades and employers alike.

Despite its apparent successes, the future was not to lie with the Populist tradition embodied by the S.R.s but with the revolutionary groups who followed the teachings of the German Socialist, Karl Marx.

Karl Marx, 1818–83

Assignment

1 Why did liberal groups oppose the autocracy?
2 What were the policies of the Union of Liberation?
3 Why did the Populists go 'to the people'?
4 How was Land and Liberty organized?
5 Outline the policies of the Socialist Revolutionary Party.

Karl Marx (1818–83)

Karl Marx was born into a Jewish family at Trier in Germany. He studied at the universities of Bonn and Berlin but was obliged to flee Germany in 1843 on account of his revolutionary ideas. He came to England in 1849 and spent the rest of his life as an exile in London, mainly studying and writing in the British Museum.

Marx's Ideas Marx believed that history was made up of a series of struggles between different classes and that the industrial revolution had brought about a situation in which the middle classes, whom he referred to as the capitalists or bourgeoisie, were engaged in a struggle with the working classes, whom he called the proletariat. The middle classes had both economic and political power. They owned the means of production – that is the land, factories, mines, railways and banks – which they ran for their own profit at the expense of the workers, whom they exploited. They controlled government and used it to prevent political and social reforms which would benefit the working classes. In 1848 he wrote:

'The history of all hitherto existing society is the history of class struggles . . . Society as a whole is more and more splitting up into two great hostile camps, into two great classes directly facing each other – bourgeoisie and proletariat.'

In place of this situation Marx wanted to establish

Socialism in which the factories, mines etc., would be controlled by the people and the profits would be used for the good of the people, instead of just making the capitalists rich.

This situation could only come about as a result of a class war in which the workers of all the industrial countries would rise up in revolt and seize power by force. This would be followed by a period of government known as the dictatorship of the proletariat, to allow the people to become politically educated enough to take full control of the government themselves. In the end the workers would control both the government and the means of production, which would be used to produce such things as better working conditions and better housing. No longer would there be any class conflict, since there would be no classes but the working class. The state would wither away and a system of Communism would be established. He wrote:

'Let the ruling class tremble at a Communist revolution. In it the proletarians have nothing to lose but their chains. They have a world to win. Working men of all countries unite!'

Marx and Russia Marx believed that the revolution would take place in one of the great industrial states of western Europe, such as Britain or Germany, where there was a large, well-established, working class. Russia, on the other hand, was a backward, peasant country with a very small industrial proletariat. This would make a revolution both difficult and unlikely. Despite Marx's pessimism there grew up within Russia revolutionary groups which adopted his views.

The Social Democrats

In 1883 a group of Russian exiles in Switzerland

George Plekhanov, 1856–1918

formed the first Russian Marxist group known as the Emancipation of Labour. It was the creation of a number of former Populists, led by George Plekhanov, who had broken with Land and Liberty over the issue of terrorism. Throughout the 1880's and 1890's Plekhanov carried on a propaganda battle with the Populists who continued to argue that Russia could by-pass capitalism, with all its horrors, and develop its own form of socialism based on the peasant commune. The Marxists argued that capitalism was necessary in Russia as it would bring about the overthrow of the autocracy. It would also give rise to an industrial proletariat which, in turn, would bring about a socialist revolution. The emphasis therefore should be shifted from the peasants to the industrial workers as the main revolutionary force.

In 1898 the various Marxist groups formed

ИСКРА

РОССІЙСКАЯ СОЦІАЛЬ-ДЕМОКРАТИЧЕСКАЯ РАБОЧАЯ ПАРТІЯ

„Изъ искры возгорится пламя!"...
Отвѣтъ декабристовъ Пушкину

№ 1.   ДЕКАБРЬ 1900 ГОДА.   № 1.

Iskra: the first issue and (below) Lenin, and other professional revolutionaries associated with the paper:

Sverdlov

Stalin

(Lenin's wife) Krupskaya

themselves into the Social Democratic Party but the movement remained disunited until 1900 when the first edition of *Iskra* – the Spark – was published. The paper was printed in various European cities and smuggled into Russia where a network of agents distributed it throughout the great industrial centres. By this time a generation of professional revolutionists, accustomed to living under a false passport, had emerged. As a later writer explains:

'The familiar cycle of secret agitation, arrest, exile, return to seditious activity in another place under another name, was known to many a revolutionist.'

None more so than to one of the editorial board of *Iskra* whose career was henceforth to dominate the development of Marxism in Russia – Vladimir Ilyich Ulyanov, known as Lenin.

Lenin

Lenin was born in 1870 at Simbrisk on the Volga. His father, a teacher of physics and mathematics, rose to be director of schools for Simbirsk province. His mother was from land-owning gentry of German stock. There were six children of whom five were to become active revolutionaries.

The eldest son, Alexander, was executed in 1887 for his part in a plot to assassinate Alexander III. The event had a profound affect on the young Lenin who was in his last year at school at the time. By the winter of 1887–8 Lenin had become a revolutionary though not yet a Marxist. He had

26

entered the University of Kazan but had been expelled for revolutionary activities and eventually graduated in law in 1891, as an external student of the University of St. Petersburg. By 1893 he had become a Marxist and moved to the capital to begin political agitation among the factory workers. In 1895, Lenin went to Switzerland to meet with Plekhanov. The older generation of Marxist exiles were impressed by this newcomer to their ranks.

Paul Axelrod wrote:

> 'I felt that I had before me a man who would be the leader of the Russian Revolution. He was not only a cultured Marxist – of them there were many – but he also knew what he wanted to do and how to do it.'

Four months later Lenin returned to Russia. The St. Petersburg Union of Struggle for the Liberation of the Working Class, which he had helped form, had been active in the strike movement of that year, and this, combined with his Geneva visit, alerted the secret police. He was arrested, imprisoned, then sentenced to administrative exile in Siberia. The time was spent studying and writing. On his release in 1900 he left Russia for Geneva and the editorial board of *Iskra*. In Lenin's eyes the paper performed two vital functions, as one historian explains:

> 'First it was to propagate . . . his ideas of a tight, centralized party; secondly, the men who smuggled it into Russia and the organizers of circles for reading it were already, by this activity, a reasonably disciplined and centralized organization. Thus Lenin for the first time, came into effective control of a grouping based on himself in Switzerland and radiating outwards into Russia.'

'What is to be done?' In 1902 Lenin published a pamphlet entitled *What is to be done?* in which he outlined the main principles of what was later to be known as Leninism. In this booklet he attacked the 'Economists' in the Party who saw the duty of the Social Democrats as supporting the workers in their trade union activity to improve wages and conditions. Lenin argued against this on the grounds that trade union leaders all too readily grew to accept middle class government. The labour movement, according to Lenin, required the leadership of a 'socialist vanguard who shall devote to the revolution not only their spare evenings, but the whole of their lives'. The idea of such a revolutionary elite owed much to the Russian traditions of Populists such as Chernyshevsky and Tkachev as well as to the early writings of Marx. Along with such leadership there must be strict discipline and centralized control by a process later known as 'democratic centralism'. Lenin wrote:

> 'All members of the factory committee must regard themselves as agents of the central committee, bound to submit to all its directions.'

Such opinions as these were to create a split in the Social Democratic Party at its second congress held in Brussels and London in 1903.

Bolsheviks and Mensheviks The basic conflict developed during the debate on the qualifications for membership of the Party. Lenin wanted to create a small party of organized and disciplined, full-time professional revolutionaries, while Julius Martov wished to create a mass party of part-time sympathizers similar to the social democratic parties of France and Germany. On this issue Lenin was defeated, but on the vote for the control of *Iskra* he received a majority. On the basis of this Lenin's followers became known as Bolsheviks

Mensheviks Paul Axelrod and Julius Martov with Martinov.

(from the Russian word for majority) while Martov and his supporters were called Mensheviks (the Russian for minority).

Lenin's views were opposed by many leading Marxists because they believed that they pointed the way towards dictatorship either by a group or by one man. Lenin's quarrel with the Mensheviks led, in the following year, to a split with Plekhanov and Lenin's resignation from *Iskra*. He started a new journal – *Forward* – and by 1905 the division between the two social democratic factions seemed complete when both Bolsheviks and Mensheviks held separate congresses. Over the years the difference between the two groups became wider.

The Bolsheviks in the Wilderness   Despite their name the Bolsheviks were in fact a minority. Apart from a brief return to Russia in 1905, Lenin remained in exile until 1917. Inside Russia the numbers of his supporters dwindled. He survived, and in the end triumphed, because he possessed greater force, energy and determination than his rivals and was prepared to sacrifice anything or anybody in the pursuit of his ideas. Potresov described him as:

'. . . a man of iron will and indomitable energy, capable of instilling fanatical faith in the movement and the cause, and possessed of equal faith in himself.'

Assignment

1 Explain what Marx meant by the following words or phrases:
   a) bourgeoisie
   b) proletariat
   c) means of production
   d) class war
   e) socialism
2 Why did Marx think it unlikely that there would be a revolution in Russia?
3 What was the function of *Iskra* in Lenin's eyes?
4 Describe the type of revolutionary party Lenin wished to create.
5 Explain how the terms 'Bolshevik' and 'Menshevik' came about.

Chapter Four

The Revolution of 1905

Unrest at Home

Russia in the first years of the century experienced a wave of unrest and disorder. In the countryside peasants seized land, burned buildings and organized boycotts. In the industrial centres of

In this satirical cartoon the Tsar is shown as the Angel of Peace while his soldiers murder innocent people

Odessa and Kiev and the oil towns of Tiflis and Batum there was an outbreak of strikes, which led to mass meetings and demonstrations which became so large that the police and military were unable to control them. In the universities there was widespread unrest, especially among students belonging to national minorities such as Poles and Ukranians, and increasing political agitation, which showed itself in the assassination of two government ministers by student revolutionaries.

It was against this background that Minister of the Interior, Plehve, organized ruthless attacks on the Jewish communities by organizations such as The Black Hundreds, in an attempt to divert hostility away from the government and towards the Jews. He also hoped to turn the attention of the Russian people away from the country's internal problems and towards an external threat posed by a foreign power. He put his case to Minister of War, Kuropatkin: 'In order to hold back the revolution we need a small victorious war.'

On the night of 8 February 1904 his hopes were realized when, without warning, Japanese warships struck the Russian squadron anchored in the harbour of Port Arthur in southern Manchuria.

Gathering Storms Abroad

Russian interest in the Far East had increased after 1891 with the decision to build a Trans-Siberian Railway. Minister of Finance, Witte, believed that the railway would enable Russia to make inroads into the vast Chinese market as well as open up Siberia to settlers. He also hoped that a considerable share of the trade conducted between the Far East and Europe could be carried by the railway thus bringing large profits to Russia through freight charges. Russian naval planners also had interests in the area. Vladivostok on the Pacific coast is ice-bound for part of the year and the acquisition of an ice-free port in Korea or northern China was felt to be desirable.

This interest in the Far East brought Russia into conflict with Japan which had begun to look towards Korea and Manchuria as a source of raw materials and as an area on which to settle Japan's surplus rural population. In 1894 Japan fought a brief war with China in which Korea was occupied and the Liaotung Peninsula, Manchuria's outlet to the sea, was demanded from the Chinese authorities. The following year Russia, with the help of France and Germany, was able to put pressure on the Japanese to give up these gains.

Russian Advances in the Far East In 1896 Russia signed a treaty with China. A new railway was to be built across northern Manchuria linking Vladivostok with Siberia by the shortest possible route. This Chinese Eastern Railway and the immediate area through which it passed was to be administered and policed by the Russians. In 1895 a further concession was wrung from the Chinese – the Liaotung Peninsula and Port Arthur was ceded to the Russians for twenty-five years and a South Manchurian Railway built from Harbin on the Chinese Eastern Line to Port Arthur. This increased the desire of the Russian navy to gain control of a Korean Port as Japanese control of the Straits of Tsushima threatened Russian links between Port Arthur and Vladivostok.

At the turn of the century all the great powers were attempting to take advantage of China's

The Russo-Japanese war, 1904–5

weakness and, in 1900 Chinese hostility to this exploitation resulted in the Boxer Rebellion. Troops were sent by foreign powers to crush this rebellion and Russia took advantage of the situation by occupying most of Manchuria.

In 1903 Witte was dismissed from the Ministry of Finance which had previously controlled Russian operations in the Far East. The Tsar set up a new command in the area under Admiral Alexeyev responsible to Nicholas alone. The Tsar became involved with a group of shady speculators who urged an expansionist policy in the East, and the confusion and indecision which existed in St. Petersburg hastened the drift to war. This forward policy was opposed both by Minister of War, Kuropatkin and by Witte who wrote:

'An armed clash with Japan in the near future . . . will cost us too much and will badly injure the country economically. Furthermore, . . . in the

Tsar Nicholas blesses his troops before they go to war

eyes of the Russian people a war with Japan for the possession of distant Korea will not be justified and the latent dissatisfaction may render more acute the alarming phenomena of our domestic life, which make themselves felt even in peace time.'

By 1904 the Japanese had had enough of Russian policy in the Far East. The Russians had agreed to withdraw all their troops from Manchuria by February 1903 but had failed to do so. The Japanese, having secured the support of Britain by an alliance in 1902, decided on war.

The Russo-Japanese War The initial attack by the Japanese on Port Arthur was followed by a series of engagements, between Admiral Togo and the Russian fleet, which were largely indecisive. It was only in mid-April 1904 that the balance shifted. The Russian naval commander, Admiral Makarov, was lost with most of his crew when his flagship, the *Petropavlovsk*, hit a Japanese mine. Makarov's

successors were too timid to leave Port Arthur and the Japanese gained mastery of the sea. They were now able to start the war in earnest. They pursued two lines of attack; the first, a push through Korea across the Yalu River into Manchuria towards the key railway junction of Mukden and the second, a direct landing on the Liaotung Peninsula to cut off Port Arthur and lay siege to it.

The Russians, under Kuropatkin who had resigned his ministry to take command, fought two major battles to try to relieve Port Arthur. But at both the ten-day battle at Liao-Yang in August/ September and the twelve-day battle on the Sha Ho River in October the Russians were forced to retreat with heavy losses. On 2 January 1905 Port Arthur surrendered to General Nogi after a direct siege of 156 days – although it was widely believed that the garrison could have fought on, being forced to surrender by the incompetence and cowardice of its commander, General Stoessel.

An attack on the Japanese positions south-west

The naval battle for Port Arthur: a Japanese view

of Mukden in late January 1905 achieved nothing but 12,000 Russian casualties and merely set the scene for the biggest battle of the war – the two-week struggle for Mukden which took place at the end of February. Over 600,000 troops were involved and the battle ended with both armies intact except for very heavy casualties (90,000 Russian – 70,000 Japanese) but with the Japanese in possession of Mukden.

The Battle of Tsushima The final Russian humiliation took place on 27 May 1905. The Russian Baltic Fleet had sailed from Kronstadt in October 1904 to join with the squadron in Port Arthur and to drive the Japanese from the seas. Having sailed half-way around the world, Admiral Rozhestvensky brought his fleet of largely old, slow, ships into the China Seas. The Port Arthur Fleet was gone and Rozhestvensky decided to push on to Vladivostok taking the direct route through the Straits of Tsushima (which separate Korea from

Japan) rather than make a wide sweep east of Japan.

Here, in under an hour, Admiral Togo blew the Russians out of the water. Twenty Russian ships were sunk; five surrendered; six were interned in neutral ports and only two cruisers and two minelayers reached Vladivostok. The speed of the Japanese ships combined with the accuracy of their gunnery accounted for most of the Russian losses.

This disaster, together with the growing spread of revolutionary activity inside Russia, convinced the Tsar of the need to end the war. The Japanese, although victorious on land and sea, were approaching the end of their resources of materials and manpower and agreed to the offer of President Theodore Roosevelt to mediate.

The Treaty of Portsmouth The peace conference was held in August 1905 in Portsmouth, New Hampshire, U.S.A., with Witte leading the Russian delegation. Under the terms of the Treaty:

1 Russia recognized Korea as a Japanese sphere of influence.
2 The Liaotung Peninsula and the South Manchurian Railway went to Japan.
3 Northern Manchuria and the Chinese Eastern Railway remained under Russian control.
4 The island of Sakhalin was divided into two.

Reasons for the Russian Defeat The Russians badly underestimated the Japanese. Since the restoration of the Emperor in 1860 the Japanese had rapidly built up the machinery of warfare and had developed the techniques and the skilled manpower to use it.

The Japanese had control of the sea and had relatively short lines of supply and communication. The Russians had to move troops and equipment along the 8,000 km. length of the single-track Trans-Siberian Railway which was not yet completed. There was a gap of over 160 km. at Lake Baikal and all men and material had to be off loaded and carried by boats to the rail link on the other side.

The viceroy, Admiral Alexeyev, was Commander-in-Chief of the whole Far Eastern theatre but General Kuropatkin was placed in command of the armies. Bad relations between the two men and the issuing of contradictory orders contributed to Russian difficulties.

There were equipment problems. The Russian soldiers frequently lacked suitable and adequate food, clothing and housing.

Assignment

1 What evidence is there of growing unrest inside Russia at the start of the century?
2 What solutions did the Minister of the Interior offer for diverting the agitation?
3 Why did Japan and Russia come into conflict in the Far East?
4 Outline the main events of the Russo-Japanese War.
5 What losses did Russia suffer by the Treaty of Portsmouth?
6 What reasons can you suggest for the Russian failure in the war against Japan?

The Impact of the Russo-Japanese War

The outbreak of war against Japan had met with a mixed reception but the Government did much to encourage patriotic feelings by organizing a number of pro-war demonstrations. It also restricted the numbers of men called up from towns and industrial centres, in an attempt to quieten the opposition. Only in border areas such as Finland, Poland and the Caucasus was there open hostility to the war but with the news of mounting military defeats in the East, unrest spread throughout the rest of Russia.

Demonstrations and disorders were reported from Warsaw, Riga and Baku. The Governor of Finland and the hated Minister of the Interior, Plehve, were assassinated by socialist revolutionary combat squads.

The newly formed Union of Liberation, led by Paul Milyukov, organized anti-government meetings throughout the country at which they demanded the abolition of the autocracy, the setting up of a parliament, universal suffrage and freedom of the press, religion and assembly.

In December 1904 the Tsar issued a royal edict in which he promised some minor reforms but made no mention of elected representatives in government. He then made matters worse by telling the *zemstva* and the Union of Liberation to mind their own business and to stop interfering in

Father Gapon

Putilov workers on strike, 1905

areas where they had no legal rights. Despite this restatement of the Tsar's absolute power, events were soon to show the real weaknesses of the autocracy.

Father Gapon and the Putilov Strike

In early January 1905 a strike had broken out in the Putilov iron works in St. Petersburg. Four workers had been sacked for belonging to the Assembly of St. Petersburg Factory Workers. This organization had been set up by a former police agent, Father Georgy Gapon, an Orthodox priest. Gapon, following in the traditions of Zubatov, had been asked by the authorities to direct the workers' grievances towards economic reform and away from political agitation. Fearing that the Assembly would lose support from the workers if he did not take action, Gapon took up the case of the dismissed workmen. He appealed to the Putilov management, to the local factory inspector and even to the Governor of St. Petersburg to get the men reinstated, but with no success. He then organized a strike. The whole

Putilov workforce came out in sympathy. Within a few days they were joined by 110,000 others from almost every factory in the city. As the strike spread Gapon had the idea of a personal appeal to the Tsar over the heads of the factory owners and government ministers.

Faced with a virtual general strike in the capital the authorities took action. By 20/21 January troops were posted at electricity stations, gas works, telephone exchanges, railway stations, the State Bank and the major factories. Special detachments guarded the area around the Winter Palace and the road junctions which linked the city centre with the working class districts.

Gapon's Petition Gapon drew up a petition outlining the workers' sufferings and demands:

'Sire, we workers and residents of the city of St. Petersburg, our wives, children and helpless old parents, have come to you, our ruler, to seek justice and protection.'

The petition then went on to ask for:
1 An 8-hour day and freedom to organize trade unions.
2 Improved working conditions, free medical aid, higher wages for women workers.
3 Elections to be held for a constituent assembly by universal, equal and secret suffrage.
4 Freedom of speech, press, association and religion.
5 An end to the war with Japan.

Gapon gave notice of the march, emphasizing its peaceful nature, to the Tsar and to the new Minister of the Interior, Mirsky. He received no reply. The Tsar's diary entry for the 21 January reads:

'There was much activity and many reports. Fredericks came to lunch. Went for a long walk. Since yesterday all the factories and workshops in St. Petersburg have been on strike. Troops have been brought in from the surroundings to strengthen the garrison. The workers have conducted themselves calmly hitherto. Their number is estimated at 120,000. At the head of the workers' union some priest – socialist Gapon. Mirsky came in the evening with a report of the measures taken.'

The Tsar then left the Winter Palace and the city to join his family at Tsarskoye Selo.

Bloody Sunday On Sunday 22 January, from mid-morning onwards, the workers assembled at various points on the outskirts of the city, then moved in groups towards the centre. They wore their Sunday best, brought their wives and children, carried holy icons, religious banners and portraits of the Tsar. They sang hymns and the

Bloody Sunday: the march to the Winter Palace

national anthem. Some 200,000 in all, divided into five columns, led by Gapon in his priestly vestments, converged on the square before the Winter Palace. They found the road barred by police and infantry with Cossack cavalry drawn up in front. The crowd were ordered to disperse but still they came on. An observer described the scene:

'The Cossacks at first used their knouts, then the flats of their sabres, and finally they fired. The strikers in the front ranks fell on their knees and implored the Cossacks to let them pass, protesting they had no hostile intentions. . . . The people seeing the dead and dying carried away in all directions, snow on the streets and the pavements soaked with blood cried for vengeance.'

Bloody Sunday: troops open fire on the crowd

The infantry joined in and massacres took place all over St. Petersburg, soldiers firing volley after volley into men, women and children too tightly packed to escape. There were at least a thousand casualties. All of Russia was aroused by 'Bloody Sunday' and the forces of revolution rapidly gained in strength. That evening the Tsar noted:

> 'A painful day. There have been serious disorders in St. Petersburg because workmen wanted to come up to the Winter Palace. Troops had to open fire in several places in the city; there were many killed and wounded. God, how painful and sad.'

The Effects of Bloody Sunday Throughout 1905 unrest mounted among all sections of Russian society. Strikes continued in various parts of the country and involved for the first time many groups of workers, bakers, cabmen, harbour workers, who had not engaged in strike activity before. The universities closed down as the whole student body staged a walkout demanding civil liberties and a constituent assembly. Political assassinations continued and in February, the Grand Duke Sergei, uncle of the Tsar and military governor of Moscow, was murdered. Throughout May and June a nationalist uprising took place in Poland which was only put down by the arrival of 250,000 Russian troops. The various middle class organizations of lawyers, doctors, and engineers, joined together in May in the Union of Unions and demanded a constituent assembly. In June a delegation from the *zemstvo* congress approached the Tsar and asked for elections to be held for a national assembly. The Tsar gave no definite reply but banned all future *zemstvo* conferences. That same summer saw an increase in disturbances in the countryside. There were rent and labour strikes and the illegal cutting of timber and illegal grazing of livestock, but as yet little arson or land seizure. A Peasants Union was formed to co-ordinate the rural movement and draw up proposals for the transfer of land.

Assignment

1 Give examples of the unrest which swept Russia during 1905.
2 Why had Father Gapon organized a strike at the Putilov iron works?
3 What evidence can you put forward to support the claim that the march to the Winter Palace was intended to be peaceful?
4 In your own words describe how the authorities dealt with the march.
5 How did the Tsar react to the news of Bloody Sunday?

The Potemkin Mutiny

In June 1905 mutiny broke out in the Black Sea Fleet, primarily on the battleship *Potemkin*. The sailors had protested against an issue of rotten meat and their officers decided to shoot the ringleaders. The firing-squad refused to carry out the order and joined with the rest of the crew in throwing the officers overboard. They then raised the Red Flag and sailed into Odessa harbour. The city was virtually in a state of civil war. Riots and street fighting had been going on for several days and casualties were numbered in thousands. The crew of the *Potemkin* were unable to land, however, and attempts to help the rioters by firing the ships guns proved useless. The mutineers lacked leadership

and definite plans, and feared an attack from the other ships in the fleet. Not knowing what else to do the crew sailed the *Potemkin* to Romania where they scuttled the ship and surrendered themselves to the local authorities.

The October Manifesto

There was a lull in August. The strike movement seemed to be in decline, peace had been made with Japan and the middle classes were confused by the announcement of a consultative assembly or *Duma* – a kind of parliament – with very limited powers elected by an extremely restricted franchise.

The respite was short lived. In late September the Moscow printers went on strike. Cossacks were brought in and the strike spread throughout Moscow. The St. Petersburg printers came out in sympathy. The railwaymen then called a general strike on 20 October which paralysed the whole Russian railway network. Factory workers and professional men joined in throughout the country. For the first time Tsarism was faced with the combined opposition of all sections of society. Witte, returning to Russia from signing the Treaty of Portsmouth found:

> '. . . almost all traffic on the streets had ceased, street lighting was no more, . . . water supplies were cut off, the telephone network was out of action. . . . The ruler . . . was in Peterhof and communication with him was only possible by means of crown steamer. . . . The government had lost its power to act, everybody was either doing nothing or moving in different directions, and the authority of the regime and of its supreme bearer was completely trampled down.'

Witte was appointed Chief Minister and he advised Nicholas to make concessions. This was done on 30 October (17 October old style) in the October

The 1905 Revolution: a demonstration in St. Petersburg (above)

Witte builds the new Russian Constitution (right). It is obvious what the cartoonist thinks of it.

Manifesto which granted:
1 Freedom of conscience, speech, meeting and association.
2 Freedom from arrest without charge and imprisonment without trial.
3 That no law would go into force without the approval of the Duma.
4 That the voting qualification for the Duma would be lowered.

The Effects of the October Manifesto As Witte had rightly foreseen, the granting of a limited constitution had created a split in the opposition to the Tsar, between the middle and working classes. The right wing *zemstvo* members, industrialists and businessmen, dropped their hostility to the Tsar and formed a political association called the Octob-

38

Short-lived celebrations greeted the October Manifesto: workers carry a picture of the Tsar through the streets

Jews of all ages lie in the cemetery after a *pogrom*

rists. The various liberal groups had formed the Kadet Party and continued to press for a constituent assembly but hoped to achieve this through the Duma and turned hostile to the continuing demands of the workers. The workers themselves, who had set up a council or *soviet* in St. Petersburg to run the city during the strike, were obliged to return to work and the number of strikes decreased. In the countryside conditions grew worse. The acute land hunger of the peasants led to disorders throughout the autumn and into 1906. Manor houses were burned and estates looted and gutted. The government tried to distract the workers and peasants from revolutionary outbursts by organizing *pogroms* (mob attacks) against the Jewish communities. Thousands were killed in massacres throughout the country, from Odessa on the Black Sea to Tomsk in Siberia.

The St. Petersburg Soviet The first *Soviet* had appeared at Ivanovna – Voznesensk in the textile region near Moscow in May 1905. It had begun as a strike committee but had developed into an elected representative body of all the town's workers. The idea had taken hold during the summer and, with the strike of October, the St. Petersburg Soviet had developed when the local Menshevik group, together with the strike committees of various factories, took up the notion of an organization involving all the workers in the city. Each delegate was to represent 500 workers and inside the soviet an elected executive committee dealt with day-to-day business. The St. Petersburg Soviet formed the model for around fifty others of which the Moscow Soviet was the most significant.

The St. Petersburg Soviet met in the Technological Institute and published its own newspaper – *Izvestya*. Its first president was a lawyer, Khrustalev-Nosar but the dominant figure in the Soviet was Leon Trotsky.

Trotsky Lev Davidovitch Bronstein was born in 1879 in Yanovka, a village in the province of Kherson in the southern Ukraine, the son of a

Trotsky: a Tsarist police photo taken when he was 18

moderately wealthy Jewish farmer. He was educated in Odessa and the nearby town of Nikolayev and during his last year at school became involved with a group of former *Narodniks*. His flirtation with Populism was short lived and, under the influence of Alexandra Sekolovskaya, whom he later married, he became a Marxist. In 1897 he organized The Southern Russian Workers' Union among the dockers and factory hands of Nikolayev. He was arrested in 1899 and sentenced in 1900 to four years exile in Siberia. Here he wrote a number of essays and newspaper articles which were to earn him the nickname of 'The Pen'. In 1902 he escaped from Siberia under a false passport in the name of Trotsky (his former gaoler in Odessa) and travelled across Europe to meet with Lenin in London. Here he wrote for *Iskra* and went on lecture tours.

At the crucial 1903 Congress he sided with the Mensheviks against Lenin but later broke with them and maintained an independent position between the two groups. He returned to St. Petersburg in late October 1905 and immediately attacked the Tsar's manifesto as a short-lived gesture of paper liberty. As for the new government – he called it a 'police whip wrapped in the parchment of a constitution'.

The Failure of the Revolution The government was obliged for six weeks to put up with the St. Petersburg Soviet before it felt strong enough to move against it. On 15 November the Soviet called a second general strike as a protest against the court-martialling of naval mutineers at Kronstadt, and against the declaration of martial law in Poland and many parts of Russia. Although well supported in the capital the strike gained little support elsewhere and was called off after four days. The Soviet then attempted to enforce an 8-hour working day and the workers found themselves locked out by their employers. Many thousands became unemployed and by the end of November the Soviet had to abandon the campaign. On 9 December the Government felt strong enough to arrest Nosar, president of the Soviet. He was replaced by a group of three, headed by Trotsky. On the 15 December the Soviet called for a run on the banks and a tax strike. The government then arrested the entire executive committee of the Soviet. This action met with no resistance in St. Petersburg but in Moscow the Bolshevik-dominated Soviet called a general strike, which soon developed into an armed uprising. Street fighting went on for ten days and the revolt was only crushed by a heavy artillery bombardment of the working class districts and by the ruthlessness of the Semyonovsky Guards.

Unrest continued in the rural areas and the border regions well into 1906 when law and order was restored by a number of military expeditions sent into the interior.

A Tsarist view of the 1905 Revolution: compare this with the painting over the page.

Assignment

1 Why was the *Potemkin* mutiny so short-lived?
2 What was a Duma?
3 How effective was the strike movement of October 1905? Give details.
4 What concessions did the Tsar grant under the terms of the October Manifesto?
5 For what reasons did the 1905 revolution fail?
6 What was a Soviet?

'Bolshevik' by B. Kustodiev. A peasant strides over the symbols of Imperial Russia: a Soviet view

Chapter Five

Repression and reforms

The Duma

The October Manifesto had contained a number of promises by the Tsar concerning a *Duma* or Parliament.

'To include in the participation of the work of the Duma those classes of the population that have been until now entirely deprived of the right to vote and to extend in the future by the newly created legislative way the principles of the general right of "election".

To establish as an unbreakable rule that no law shall go into force without its confirmation by the State Duma and that the persons elected by the people shall have the opportunity for actual participation in supervising the legality of the acts of authorities appointed by us.'

Before the Duma met in May 1906, the Tsar had already broken some of the promises he had made in the October Manifesto to make sure that the new Duma would not restrict the use of his autocratic powers. He created a State Council, an upper chamber, of which half the members were to be appointed by the Tsar. He retained for himself the right to declare war, to control the Orthodox Church and to dissolve the Duma. Ministers were to be responsible to the Tsar alone and could not be removed even by a vote of censure in the Duma.

The Duma, when it met for its first sessions in the Tauride Palace, presented a strange spectacle in

The first Duma in session

Moslem delegates to the first Duma

Witte: deposed chief minister

its diversity of classes, races and national groups. This Duma was to prove short-lived. At its first session the members put forward a series of demands including a greater share in the government, the abolition of the death penalty, the release of political prisoners, the right to strike and, crucially, the confiscation of large estates.

The Tsar rejected all these demands and dissolved the Duma on the grounds that it had exceeded its competence, shown itself to be incapable of efficient work and addressed an illegal appeal to the people. This refers to the attempt by some members of the Duma to rouse the Russian people by moving to Vyborg, in Finland, and issuing the Vyborg Manifesto – a proclamation 'To the people from the people's representatives' – complaining of their dismissal.

The Second Duma The second Duma was convened in February 1907. By now the Tsar had replaced Witte by Stolypin as chief minister. This Duma lasted three months before being dissolved on trumped up charges against a Social Democratic deputy, who was accused of plotting the assassin-

ation of the Tsar and of inciting the troops to mutiny. Before this was done, however, Stolypin had changed the electoral law, in breach of the October Manifesto, so that only land-owners and wealthy town dwellers retained the right to vote. The third Duma in which right wing, deputies were in a clear majority, ran for its full term as, almost, did the fourth Duma, its activities being brought to a sudden end with the events of March 1917.

Assignment

1 In what ways had the Tsar broken the promises he had made in the October Manifesto before the meeting of the first Duma?
2 Outline the demands put forward by the first Duma.
3 On what grounds did the Tsar dismiss the first Duma?
4 What was the Vyborg Manifesto?
5 Why do you think the third and fourth Dumas survived so much longer than their predecessors?

Stolypin: new chief minister

The results of a bomb attack on Stolypin's house, 1906. Thirty people were killed or injured, including his children, but Stolypin escaped unhurt

P.A. Stolypin

The Tsar, who had long resented Witte, found an opportunity to dismiss him in April 1906. For a few months Nicholas indulged the aged Goremykin as prime minister but, in July, he turned to the recently appointed Minister of the Interior, Peter Arkadievitch Stolypin, and asked him to become Chairman of the Council of Ministers.

Stolypin's background was that of the landed, provincial gentry. After University he had entered the government service and by 1903 had risen to the rank of Governor of Saratov province, on the lower Volga. The severity of his measures in suppressing what had been a turbulent province during the disorders of 1905–6 made him notorious among the peasants but brought him to the attention of the Tsar.

On taking office Stolypin had two main objectives; to repress disorder and terrorism and to introduce far-reaching land reforms.

Stolypin and public order In mid-1906 Stolypin was faced with threatened mutinies at the naval bases of Kronstadt, Sveabord and Reval as well as in a number of army units. There were fears of a peasant uprising. St. Petersburg faced a wave of strikes and the Socialist Revolutionary combat squads had embarked on a campaign of terror and assassination from which the new first minister himself was not immune.

Stolypin met violence with violence. A number of provinces were placed under martial law and special military courts were set up to deal speedily with suspected terrorists. Over three thousand suspects were convicted and executed by these

Stolypin's measures: the shooting of strikers (left) and the repression of minority peoples: a Tsarist policeman stops Jews breaking out of the Pale of Settlement (right).

special courts between 1906–9, and the hangman's noose became popularly known as Stolypin's necktie. He displayed great calm and detachment in his policy of repression but, on occasions, he had to restrain his over-enthusiastic subordinates: 'Irregular and incautious actions which create animosity instead of restoring calm will not be tolerated.'

Stolypin was also an intense Russian nationalist and this led him to extend the policy of government repression to the various minority peoples of the Russian Empire. Poles and Jews were subject to particular harassment, and unsavoury organizations, such as the Black Hundreds, were given official encouragement for their clandestine activities. These policies brought public disorder under control but lost for the government what little there remained of popular sympathy.

Land Reforms The problems of the peasantry had rumbled on since Emancipation, but it was only after the agrarian disturbances of 1905–6, which followed on from the defeats of the Russo-Japanese war, that the government felt the need to undertake radical reforms in the Russian countryside.

The main purpose of Stolypin's reforms was to allow the peasants freely to buy and sell land by destroying the power of the village commune. This would allow a class of able peasants to develop as small land-owners. These rich peasants, or *kulaks*, would thus have a strong stake in the existing order. They would therefore tend to keep the more unruly elements in line and so stem the tide of revolution in the countryside. The poor peasants were expected to decline into landless labourers who would provide a pool of cheap labour available for work on both farm and in factory.

These new farms would do away with the strip system and give rise to enclosed units which, it was hoped, would be much more efficient and bring about a welcome increase in the yields of Russian agriculture.

Stolypin's reforms were contained in a number of acts passed between 1906 and 1911 and may be summarized as follows:

1 Every householder in a commune where the land was periodically redistributed was entitled to demand his share of land in one consolidated holding.

2 Where the land in a commune was based on hereditary tenure the government simply decreed that individual ownership was in force.

3 Joint family ownership was abolished and the family elder was to be regarded as the owner of the household's allotment.

4 Enclosures took place as the strips were consolidated into one farmstead.

5 Communally owned grazing and pasture land was divided up.

6 The Peasants Land Bank was enlarged to help the richer peasants buy out their poorer neighbours.

7 The Land Captains lost their power over the peasants.

8 The peasants were allowed to obtain passports on the same terms as anyone else, thus increasing labour mobility to the towns and allowing vast numbers to move to new settlements in western Siberia.

The Results of the Land Reforms By 1916 some two million householders had received legal title to their new lands and had started up as independent farmers. In 1913 Prince Trubetskoi wrote:

'Two new facts in particular strike the observer of the Russian countryside in recent years; the rise in the standard of material welfare and the astonishing growth of a new social order.'

While Foreign Minister Izvolsky, when he came to write his memoirs, was of the opinion that

'a considerable extension of the activity and power of the Peasants' Bank produced widespread results in a surprisingly short time. These results were so satisfactory that on the eve of the revolution of 1917 it is safe to say that the entire agrarian problem was in a way to being definitely solved.'

If Stolypin had been granted twenty years of peace the land reforms might have transformed rural Russia, but in the short term they were not by themselves enough:

1 The problem was only partly one of land redistribution. Russian agricultural techniques were so backward that the yield in crops remained low despite private ownership.

2 Stolypin's reforms took no account of the growth in rural population which greatly outstripped the amount of land made available, thus the basic problem of land hunger remained.

3 The rate of private ownership varied enormously among the various provinces of Russia, depending on the system of land tenure which had previously existed.

Industrial Developments Although Stolypin's main concern was the peasants, he did not neglect Russia's industrial development. From 1908 onwards substantial growth took place in the coal, iron and steel industries. Railway building also proceeded but not at the pace of the 1890's. At the outbreak of war in 1914 Russia was still sadly deficient in the provision of both roads and railways. However, industrial growth had created employment and there were few signs of unrest among the workers during the period 1908–14.

The Death of Stolypin Stolypin was a formidable figure in Russian political life but one who had few friends and made many powerful enemies. His appearance was forbidding:

'A tall, stiff man with a dead white face and a dead black beard. . . . He left an impression only of cold gentleness, of icy compassion, of saddened self control.'

The Duma disliked the way he crushed their

attempts to gain more power. The revolutionaries hated him because of his repressive policies; and even Lenin, in exile, was concerned in case the success of his agricultural policies brought an end to revolutionary feeling in the Russian countryside. The Tsaritsa hated him because he had exiled the unruly Rasputin, and the Tsar turned against him when he felt that Stolypin's policies threatened even his autocratic powers. The *Okhrana* therefore did nothing when they learned of a plot to murder him in 1911.

The occasion was a gala performance, at the Kiev Opera House, of Rimsky-Korsakov's opera *The Tale of Tsar Saltan*. An historian describes the events:

'Nicholas was in the Imperial box; Stolypin in the stalls. The security precautions were of the most stringent kind imaginable. They did not, however, prevent yet another of those twilight figures who blur at every turn the sharp edges of Russian history, from entering the theatre and shooting Stolypin dead. The assassin was a Jew called Bogrov, a Socialist Revolutionary turned police agent.'

Within three years of his death Russia had drifted into a war which destroyed not only any possibility of success with the peasantry, but the very dynasty which Stolypin had struggled to maintain.

Assignment

1 For what reasons did Stolypin first attract the attentions of the Tsar?
2 By what means did Stolypin stamp out civil disorder?
3 What was the main purpose of Stolypin's agrarian reforms?
4 Outline the main changes contained in Stolypin's reforms.
5 Is it fair to say that Stolypin's reforms were not sufficient to transform rural Russia? Give reasons for your answer.
6 Why do you think so many people disliked Stolypin?

Europe in 1914.

Chapter Six

Russia at war, 1914–17

Why Russia Entered World War I

Background   During most of the nineteenth century Russia had been on friendly terms with Germany, but this situation had changed by the 1890's. Chancellor Bismarck, who had always been careful to maintain friendly relations with Russia, was forced to resign in 1890, by the new Kaiser, Wilhelm II.

Austria-Hungary, the ally of Germany, wished to increase her influence in the Balkans, where many small nations were scrambling for independence as the Turkish Empire disintegrated and gradually withdrew from Europe. Russia had historic rights in this region to protect the Christian subjects of the Turkish Sultan, but Russian interest was not confined to matters of race and religion. Russia had long sought the opening to her warships of the Straits which linked the Black Sea to the Aegean, but international pressure had always prevented this.

The result was that Russia drew apart from Germany and Austria-Hungary and in 1894 made a military alliance with France. The Dual Alliance was strengthened in 1907 when Russia attempted to settle her differences with Britain with whom France already had made an Entente in 1904. Britain however, had no military alliance with either Russia or France.

The Annexation of Bosnia   In 1908 Austria-Hungary annexed the former Turkish provinces of Bosnia and Herzegovina. The Russians agreed to this move but wished, as compensation, to be permitted to bring warships out of the Black Sea. To this, they believed, the Austrians had agreed. However, no other European power would agree to a revision of the Straits Convention, and Russian attempts to bring about an international conference to compensate Serbia for the Austrian annexation of Bosnia also came to nothing. Russia could only press her claims at the risk of a general war and, given the unpreparedness of the Russian Army after its defeats at the hands of the Japanese, she had no alternative but to back down. At the insistence of Germany, Russia was also obliged to put pressure on Serbia to abandon its claims for compensation and to give assurances of good behaviour towards Austria-Hungary. It now became the aim of Russia to prevent, by all diplomatic means, any further Austrian moves into the Balkans.

The Balkan Wars 1912–13   Russia was drawn into support for a Balkan alliance against Turkey but, although militarily successful, Russia's ally Serbia was prevented by the Austrians, at the peace conference, from gaining the Albanian coast and thus access to the Adriatic Sea. The victors quarrelled over the division of the area known as Macedonia and a second Balkan War broke out. This resulted in the emergence of a strong independent Serbia which Austria regarded as a threat to the security of her Empire, as it provided a rallying point for the discontented Slavs under Austrian rule.

The Assassination at Sarajevo   On the 28 June 1914, the Archduke Franz-Ferdinand, heir to the throne of the Austro-Hungarian Empire was assassinated by Gavrilo Princip in the Bosnian capital of Sarajevo. The Austrian government decided to make use of this opportunity by claiming Serbian involvement in the killing. An ultimatum was sent to Serbia whose inevitable rejection gave the Austrians the justification they sought to invade and destroy Serbia. Russia was put in the position of either abandoning Serbia for the third time in five years or asserting her claims as the ally and defender of the Balkan Slav people. She decided to mobilize her armies and, despite a series of last minute telegrams between the Kaiser and Tsar Nicholas, war was declared on 1 August 1914.

The Eastern Front in 1914

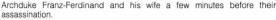
Archduke Franz-Ferdinand and his wife a few minutes before their assassination.

Russia at War

The Invasion of East Prussia   The War began with the German attack on France through Belgium in accordance with the long prepared Schlieffen Plan. In order to take pressure off their allies, the French, two Russian armies invaded the German territory of East Prussia. The army of the Niemen under General Rennenkampf attacked towards Konigsberg, while a second army under General Samsonov attacked northwards from Poland. Both armies were separated by the lakes and marshlands of Masuria.

The Germans had assumed that the slow

The Russian Commanders: Samsonov (left) and Rennenkampf (right).

moving Russian military machine would take six weeks to mobilize and reach the frontier and had therefore left only a light force to guard the eastern borders. The speed and success of Rennenkampf's advance obliged the Germans to quickly redirect forces to the east. The Kaiser appointed Field Marshal Paul von Hindenburg as Commander-in-Chief with General Erich von Ludendorff as his Chief-of-Staff. Two German divisions were taken from the western front thereby significantly weakening the German forces in the west, to the extent that Paris was saved and the French achieved victory on the Marne.

Hindenburg decided to allow Rennenkampf to continue his advance and to concentrate his own numerically smaller forces first against the army of Samsonov.

The German Commanders: Hindenburg and Ludendorff.

The Battle of Tannenberg The rapid and successful advance into East Prussia disguised some of the basic weaknesses of the Russian position. They lacked adequate maps to enable them to make a sustained move through the forests, lakes and marshes of the region. Their military intelligence was poor and they used no code for their wireless messages, allowing the Germans to easily monitor their movements. Rennenkampf and Samsonov, largely for personal reasons, neither communicated nor co-operated. Samsonov did not learn until too late that his main line of retreat and supply was cut off and that the Germans had sealed in his army on three sides. Hindenburg, on the other hand was able to keep himself supplied by rail, and to command civilian transport to bring thousands of men by road to the scene of the battle. The Russians had superiority in men but the Germans were superior in the essential departments of modern warfare – heavy artillery, high explosive shells, hand grenades and plenty of machine-guns.

The Battle of Tannenberg lasted three days. The Germans took over 100,000 prisoners and large quantities of guns. Three Russian army corps were all but destroyed. By the evening of 29 August, General Samsonov knew the extent of the catastrophe which had befallen his army. He slipped away from his escort into the forest, where the Germans found his corpse two days later with a single bullet hole through the head.

The Battle of the Masurian Lakes Hindenburg, now strengthened by reinforcements arriving from the west, regrouped his forces and launched an attack against Rennenkampf's left flank on 5 September. Rennenkampf held off the German assault at the centre, but in so doing weakened the whole of his army. On 9 September he ordered a general withdrawal, to pull the 1st Army out of the trap closing on it. His army did escape but with 100,000

Tannenberg: Russian prisoners after the battle

men lost. 'The invasion of Prussia, which had cost the Russians almost a quarter of a million men, had failed.'

By the end of September 1914, the Germans had regained all the territory lost in the first Russian onslaught.

Assignment

1 What interests did Russia have in the Balkans and why did this bring her into conflict with Austria-Hungary?
2 For what reasons did Russia go to war in 1914?
3 In what ways did France benefit from the Russian attack on East Prussia?
4 Outline the military advantages enjoyed by the Germans during the campaign in East Prussia.
5 Give details of the extent of the Russian defeats of Tannenberg and the Masurian Lakes.

Galicia 1914 In the south-west the Russian armies had greater success against the Austrians. Galicia was invaded and the Austrians forced to retreat. Lemberg (Lvov), the provincial capital and a major railway junction, was captured in September 1914. The Russians then crossed the Carpathian Mountains thus directly threatening Vienna and the Danube plain. The Austrians appealed to Germany for help and they attacked the Russians, in late September, from Silesia. The Russians counter-attacked in East Prussia only to be driven back towards Warsaw in November by German forces under Von Makensen. However, the offensive in Galicia was halted and the chance of a speedy victory over the Austrians was lost.

German Counter-attack May 1915 In March 1915 Russian Armies under General Brusilov, swollen by two million raw recruits, again attacked through Galicia and reached the Carpathians. The

Galicia: Russian soldiers retreat

Germans, fearful that Italian entry into the war would place an unbearable burden onto the Austrians, decided to strike a decisive blow against the Russians, Austria's main enemy, before the Italians came into action. In May, a well-prepared German offensive under General Makensen, backed by massed artillery and air attacks, broke through the Russian lines at Gorlice. It was at this point that the lack of preparation for war by the Russians showed itself most acutely. Untrained troops were thrown into battle without arms or ammunition, obliged to wait on the death of a comrade to obtain a rifle. The Russians fell back on all fronts. By the end of September they had lost all the Austrian territory gained in 1914 as well as Lithuania, Poland and large tracts of White Russia. This disorderly flight rapidly demoralized the army. The number of desertions and voluntary surrenders to the enemy increased. The Russians suffered almost two million casualties with a further million made prisoner.

The Refugee Problem　The Russian High Command decided on a 'scorched earth' policy in the wake of the army's retreat, in an attempt to repeat the events of 1812 when Napoleon had been lured on to Moscow to his ruin. This decision to turn Galicia into a desert resulted in chaos and catastrophe.

An observer wrote:

'Men and women are torn from their homes and are forced into the unknown. In their presence fire is set to their stocks of grain and not unfrequently to their cottages. . . . The immense stream of uprooted, desperate, suffering humanity rolls along the roads interfering with military traffic and completely disorganizing the rear of the army . . . this flood of humanity spreads over all Russia, adds to war-time hardships, creates a shortage of foodstuffs, increases the cost of living, and accentuates the discontent which is nowhere lacking . . .'

The Brusilov Offensive of 1916　In August 1915, the Tsar himself took over as Commander-in-Chief, leaving the Tsaritsa in charge of the government in St. Petersburg, now renamed Petrograd. Alexandra's conduct of the government was to prove a major factor in bringing about the revolutionary events of 1917.

By 1916 the Russian Army had partially recovered. Reinforcements had been called up and more guns and ammunition were being produced. In June, General Brusilov was put in charge of a major Russian offensive against the Austrians in Galicia. The aims were to bolster the morale of the army and population at home by a victory at last, to force the Germans to withdraw troops from the Battle of the Somme, and to relieve Austrian pressure on the Italians in the Tyrol. The Russians had early successes. They again reached the crest of the Carpathians, took some 400,000 Austrians prisoner and helped persuade the Romanians to enter the war on the Allied side. The Germans sent troops to help the Austrians and Brusilov's offensive petered out into inconclusive trench warfare, as the German artillery again took its toll.

War weariness was growing. It is true that the greatest losses had been incurred in 1915, but they were still bitterly felt in 1916. According to a later estimate, total Russian casualties, including the year 1917, were 1,300,000 killed in battle; 4,200,000 wounded, of whom 350,000 died from their wounds; and 2,417,000 prisoners. Most of these casualties were incurred before the end of 1916.

Assignment

1 Why were the Russians unable to crush the Austrians in late 1914?
2 For what reasons did the Germans attack the Russians in May 1915?
3 Why were the Russian casualties so heavy in 1915?
4 What was the purpose of the 'scorched earth' policy in Galicia?
5 What effect did the refugee problem have on the rest of Russia?

Reasons for the Failure of the Russian Army

The Commanders On the outbreak of war in 1914 the Tsar appointed his uncle, the Grand Duke Nicholas, as Commander-in-Chief. This came as a surprise to many, not least to the Grand Duke himself, who 'appeared to be a man entirely unequipped for the task'. However he was very popular with the rank and file of the army – possibly because of the severity of his treatment of the officers beneath him.

His two main subordinates were the Chief-of-Staff, General Yanushkevich and the Quartermaster General, General Danilov. Neither were ideally suited for the tasks which confronted them. Yanushkevich had seen no service in the field – 'He gave the impression rather of a courtier than of a soldier' and Danilov, nicknamed the 'Black' was 'a stern, silent man, a great disciplinarian and an exacting chief'. The failures of these commanders through 1914 and 1915 brought pressure from the government for their dismissal but they were defended by the Grand Duke – even to the Tsar.

Grand Duke Nicholas with the Tsar at the Eastern Front.

Russian army officers relax

Officers and Men   The Russian Army had many excellent lower ranking officers but the training and appointment of those in senior positions worried many Russians. One complained:

'It is . . . neither gallantry, nor genius, nor knowledge, nor experience in military art as proved in action that determine promotions, but external considerations. Under these conditions . . . gifted military leaders capable of leading us to victory seldom have reached the higher commands.'

The Russian Army was poorly organized, badly armed and equipped, and directed by commanders who mingled ignorance with incompetence. The rank and file peasant soldier was little better than those set above him. The uneducated Russian peasant population never understood why it fought. It fought well under competent leadership and in favourable circumstances, but, in the opinion of Knox, a British General at the time, 'A higher type of human animal was required to persevere to victory through the monotony of disaster.'

Tactics   The Minister of War in 1914 was Vladimir Sukhomlinov. His attitude to the military technical improvements of the previous quarter of a century was one of contempt based on a profound ignorance.

Sukhomlinov believed that an army only required the essential qualities of spirit and aggressiveness. The Russian 'steam roller' – the masses of peasant soldiers – only required a bayonet and the support of Cossack cavalry. As a consequence the Russian Army entered the war deficient in rifles, machine-guns and heavy artillery.

Lack of Equipment   At the outbreak of war Russia possessed sixty batteries of artillery against Germany's three hundred and eighty-one, and for these few guns there was an acute shortage of shells. On numerous occasions during 1914 and 1915 the infantry was sent into battle without artillery support.

The main problem however was that Russia lacked the industrial base to manufacture arms and munitions sufficient to keep such a huge army

The Russian 'steam roller'

equipped for battle. By December 1914, 6,553,000 men had been mobilized but only 4,652,000 rifles were available and this shortage grew more acute during 1915. During Makensen's offensive rifles were changing hands at 7 roubles each as Russian soldiers bartered among themselves to obtain some protection in battle. The Tsar, as Commander-in-Chief, despaired: 'If we should have three days of serious fighting we might run out of ammunition altogether.'

Failings of the Medical Service Shortages were not confined to guns. The lack of boots, warm underwear, and sheepskin coats caused many soldiers to suffer from frost-bite. If wounded in battle the soldier was faced with a shortage of first aid supplies and a lack of horses and wagons to transport him to hospital. If he reached hospital he might not get in. Observers spoke of trains of wounded without straw, without clothing, badly bandaged and lacking food, being abandoned in railway stations to be attended only by civilian volunteer nurses and doctors.

Transport In 1914 Russia possessed only 68,200 km. of railway and that was largely concentrated in Poland and western Russia. This gave rise to enormous difficulties in transporting troops and supplies to the front, especially after some 4,800 km. of track were lost after the German advance into Poland. Motor transport was almost non-existent in Russia and goods had to be transported to the front by horse and wagon along unpaved roads. The unreliability of this form of transport, particularly in winter, explains, in part, the reasons for the shortages of equipment at the front.

The major cause of these shortages was, as we have seen, a lack of industry to produce the goods. This situation was made worse by Russia's virtual isolation from the rest of the world for most of the war, as a result of the Turkish presence on the German side which closed the Straits to Russian and Allied shipping. The failure of the British expedition at Gallipoli continued their isolation.

The shortages which affected the army, the heavy losses and the repeated military disasters had by 1917 totally undermined the spirit of the army, but the war had also brought severe hardships and a subsequent loss of morale to the civilian population. Discontent at the front was to fuse with the unrest at the rear to produce the revolutionary events of March 1917.

Assignment

1 What criticisms were made of the ordinary Russian peasant as a soldier?
2 For what reasons was Russia ill prepared to fight a modern war?
3 What reasons are suggested for Russia's chronic shortage of munitions?
4 Summarize the failings of the Russian Army medical service.
5 What transport problems afflicted the Russian Army?

Chapter Seven

The Internal effects of the War

Economic Problems

Transport Russia depended heavily on imports of raw materials to supply her industries, but with the outbreak of war 87 per cent of these imports could no longer reach Russia as the western frontier was closed, the Germans blockaded the Baltic Sea and the Turks made the Dardanelles impassable. Only through the ice-bound ports of Murmansk and Archangel on the White Sea and through Vladivostok on the Pacific could supplies reach Russia from her allies. The railway links from these ports to the industrial centres were hopelessly inadequate to carry the volume of goods required. Also, as we have seen, the demands of the Army meant that the railways were often not available for civilian needs. As a result, there was little transport to deliver food to the towns and raw materials to industry. The situation became worse, after 1915, with the German capture of important locomotive works in Poland and in the Baltic regions, which resulted in a decline in the numbers of locomotives, wagons and carriages in service.

Inflation With the effective blockade of Russia, foreign trade was severely reduced and the government suffered from a loss of customs duties, while the army's use of the railways meant a loss of revenue from civilian traffic. On top of this, at the outbreak of war, the government had banned the sale of vodka, which was heavily taxed, thus further reducing its income. The government had to in-crease its spending to meet the cost of fighting the war, and new taxes were introduced and loans were raised. But these were insufficient to meet the increased expenditure, so the government resorted to printing more money which caused inflation and a rapid rise in the cost of living.

Agriculture The war increased the demand for food, and production increased in 1914 and 1915. By 1916, however, cereal production had fallen 20 per cent below the pre-war average.

This was partly as a result of a shortage of manpower. Some 15.5 million men were conscripted into the Russian army and the bulk of these were peasants; while the requisitioning by the army of horses and draught animals caused further problems in certain areas. But these were not the main reasons for the decline in output. The income of the peasants had increased with the rise in demand and the rise in the prices of agricultural products, while the absence of vodka meant that there was even more money available in the countryside. Industry, however, could not produce the tools, machinery and fertilizers which the peasants required. Therefore the peasants had little interest in trading with the towns for payment in paper money which bought little and rapidly lost value. The area sown declined.

Industry The rate of conscription also caused problems for industry. With 37 per cent of the adult males at war, increasing numbers of women, children, refugees and prisoners of war had to be employed. The mobilization of skilled workers created difficulties as the army was reluctant to provide exemptions for key men in the factories and mines. The working day was lengthened and the number of overtime hours increased, to compensate for the decline in the productivity of labour; and, although wages rose, they did not keep pace with inflation.

The Impact on the People

The Cities The reluctance of the peasants to sell to the towns, combined with the inability of the railways to perform the double task of supplying both the army and the civilian population, led to a reduction in the supply of all basic foodstuffs to the city. Prices rose, thus causing an increase in the cost of living.

Fuel was another problem. Prior to 1914 Petrograd, for example, had obtained a large part of its coal supply from Britain by way of the Baltic. By 1915 this was no longer possible and Russia's cities had to be supplied from the mines in the Donets Basin, which proved unable to produce enough to meet the demand. This situation was made worse by the inevitable transport problems. Firewood also was in short supply and was frequently requisitioned for the railways.

All this was made worse by the rapid growth of the urban population during the war years. This was a result of a number of factors:

1 Peasants moving from the countryside into city barracks as soldiers.
2 Huge labour forces being employed in the war industries.
3 Large numbers of sick and wounded soldiers being returned to hospitals.

A war-time bread queue in Petrograd

4 Thousands of refugees flooding in from the occupied areas.

This created additional pressure on the scarce food and fuel supplies, pushed up prices faster and created an acute housing shortage.

The Workers During the war the government ran most large factories under military law. Strikers were arrested, exiled or sent to the front. Trade unions were banned. Despite these measures the number of strikes rose with each year of the war. Although some of these strikes were political in intent, the influence of revolutionary groups was very slight: most strikes were economic, concerned with wages, conditions and hours of work. These became more intense after mid-1916 when the cost of living overtook wage increases. The seriousness of the situation is illustrated by a police report of October 1916:

'the industrial proletariat of the capital is on the verge of despair . . . the mass of industrial workers are quite ready to let themselves go to the wildest excesses of a hunger riot.'

Assignment

1 Outline the difficulties facing Russian industry during World War I.
2 Why did the cost of living rise so quickly at this time?
3 a) What problems did the population of Russia's cities face during the War?
  b) What reasons can you find for the shortages?
4 For what reasons were the industrial workers becoming increasingly discontented?

Political Difficulties

The declaration of war in 1914 had, for a short time, united the Russian people behind the Tsar. This enthusiasm for the monarchy was not to last as it soon became apparent that the Tsar and, more particularly, his wife were determined to preserve intact the privileges and power of the monarchy – even at the cost of Russia's war effort.

Government Action The working class were made resentful by the banning of trade unions and the arrest of all those who agitated for improved wages or conditions of work; while all revolutionary groups were suppressed, including the Bolshevik members of the Duma who were exiled to Siberia.

The government next lost the support of the middle classes. The Duma had set up a committee, under its President, Rodzianko, to deal with first aid, relief for the wounded and army supplies. The *zemstva* and the local authorities set up an organization – *Zemgor* – to tackle the problem of refugees, provide hospitals, food and transport. War industries committees were set up with representatives from both owners and workers, to try to reorganize industry to meet the needs of the armed forces. The government only reluctantly agreed to the existence of these groups as it was against all independent initiatives and organizations, which it regarded as threats to the power of the Crown. Unable to organize the country for war itself the government was not prepared to let others try.

Problems with the High Command The government, already widely criticized for its failure to meet the demands of war, had its influence further reduced by the activities of military headquarters. A law of July 1914 had established a military zone under the control of the Commander-in-Chief who was responsible to the Tsar alone. The civilian authorities in this area, which by 1915 included Petrograd, were under the command of the military. This created confusion and hostility between the government and the military authorities, and did much to undermine the authority and effectiveness of the civil service.

The Tsar Takes Over

The crushing military defeats of 1915, the shambles of the retreat, and the subsequent flood of wounded and refugees, brought discredit not only on the High Command but also on the Tsar and his ministers. The tragedy of Galicia prompted the Tsar into a fateful decision – to place himself at the head of the Russian armies as Commander-in-Chief. Nicholas saw his duty as emperor 'to be with his troops, and either lead them to victory, or perish with them'. The Tsaritsa and Rasputin welcomed the move for other reasons. Both had reasons to dislike the Grand Duke, and Alexandra was particularly worried that his widespread popularity, in the Army and in the country, would lead to moves to have him replace Nicholas as Tsar. The

The Tsar, with General Brusilov on his left, at army headquarters, 1916

1 His undoubted power, possibly through the use of hypnosis, to reduce the pain suffered by the young Tsarevich.
2 His religious background and his reputation as a man of God gained him the sympathy and support of the fanatically religious Tsaritsa.
3 His status in the eyes of the Imperial couple as a man of the people – uneducated and coarse, but divinely inspired and devoted to the throne – who could enable the Tsar to overcome the barrier dividing him from his subjects.

Tsar's decision was opposed by the Allied governments, the Duma, the Council of Ministers and the Army itself. They argued that any future military defeats would be blamed directly on Nicholas himself, while the already crumbling machinery of government would disintegrate completely in his absence. The Tsar would not be persuaded – he left for army headquarters at Mogilev, entrusting the running of the government to his wife, Alexandra Feodorovna.

Rasputin and the Royal Family Alexandra, an intensely religious woman, saw her duty to be in safeguarding the principles of autocracy and, by so doing, saving Russia: 'We have been placed by God on a throne and we must keep it firm and give it over to our son untouched.' She was to be aided in this task by Rasputin, whose advice she constantly pressed upon her husband: 'Hearken unto our Friend, believe him, he has your interest and Russia's at heart – it is not for nothing that God sent him to us – only we must pay more attention to what he says.'

Gregory Rasputin was a *starets* or wandering pilgrim from the province of Tobolsk in Siberia. His influence with the Royal Family stemmed from:

In the early days Rasputin's influence was not felt in public affairs, and it was only in 1911 that he came to public attention in connection with scandals involving the banishing of the Bishop of Saratov, who had once been involved in a brawl with Rasputin. His private life, involving bouts of drunkenness, interspaced with religiously inspired

Rasputin

Rasputin with some of his fashionable followers

orgies with a variety of society ladies, did little to enhance the reputation of the Royal Family which protected him.

The Rule of the Tsaritsa The Tsar, although he had reservations about Rasputin, was prepared to allow Alexandra almost a free rein in the handling of the government: 'You ought to be my eyes and ears there in the capital, while I have to stay here. It rests with you to keep peace and harmony among the ministers.' The Tsaritsa proceeded to remove from office, those ministers whom she disliked and those who seemed reluctant to have their policies directed by the 'Man of God'. A bewildering succession of the corrupt and the incompetent were appointed to high office on the authority of Rasputin. Some twenty-one ministers were dismissed in the space of fifteen months during this period of ministerial leap-frog.

The abuses carried out in the name of the Crown gave rise to rumours which spread throughout Russia. Suggestions were made concerning the relationship between Alexandra and Rasputin; Alexandra's German background was used to suggest the existence of a pro-German party at court working for the defeat of Russia. The Tsaritsa came commonly to be referred to as *Nemka* – the German woman – and popular indignation reached its height in November 1916 when Paul Milyukov, head of the Progressive Bloc in the Duma, made an attack on the government and the 'dark forces' surrounding the throne.

The Murder of Rasputin In December 1916, several members of the Russian nobility decided to assassinate Rasputin to try to prevent the name of the Royal Family being discredited further. The main conspirators were the Grand Duke Dmitri, nephew of the Tsar, Purishkevich, a conservative member of the Duma, and Prince Felix Yusupov who was related to the Tsar by marriage, and to whose house Rasputin was lured. Despite having been given food and drink containing cyanide and having apparently been shot through the heart, Rasputin was able to jump to his feet and struggle with his attacker who afterwards wrote:

'This devil, who was dying of poison, who had a bullet in the heart, must have been raised from the dead by the powers of evil.'

It took a further four shots to kill him. Then the body was taken and, according to Yusupov, 'they hurled it into the river'.

Paul Milyukov

Prince Yusupov

News of Rasputin's death was received with rejoicing throughout the country but his death made little difference politically. The Tsar, urged on by Alexandra, still refused to grant concessions and form a more democratic government: instead he kept, in office such Rasputin appointees as the Minister of the Interior, Protopopov, who was rapidly declining into insanity.

The Last Days of the Monarchy The winter of 1916–17 witnessed a number of futile plots aimed at removing Nicholas and Alexandra and replacing them by the Tsarevich, Alexis, with the Tsar's brother, The Grand Duke Michael, as regent. These conspiracies came to nothing, but illustrated the total lack of support for the Monarchy throughout Russia. By January 1917 the army commanders, aware of the rapid demoralization of their troops, were prepared to support drastic action.

Discipline at the front was holding – but desertions were increasing, and clashes between officers and troops becoming more regular. Some regiments were on the verge of mutiny and a profound weariness with the war pervaded the whole army. As early as September 1916 this report reached the government:

> 'The high cost of living and the shortage of foodstuffs from which the soldier's wives are the first to suffer, have been made known to the army by the soldiers returning from furloughs. . . The anxiety of soldiers about their families is perfectly understandable but it . . . offers a fertile ground for the spreading of both German and revolutionary propaganda.'

By February 1917 it was clear to all observers, except the Tsar and his wife, that a revolution was imminent. In Petrograd the combination of hunger, fuel shortages, military defeat, contempt for the government, administrative chaos and industrial unrest, was creating a wave of strikes and demonstrations which the authorities proved powerless to control. The destiny of Russia now lay in the streets of Petrograd.

Assignment

1 Why did the government lose the support of the middle classes?
2 What effect did the power of the Army High Command have on the efficiency of the government?
3 In what ways did Rasputin influence the policy of the Russian government during 1915–16?
4 What did the Tsaritsa see as her main duty as ruler?
5 Why had the Russian Army become so demoralized by early 1917?

Chapter Eight

The Revolution of March 1917

Background

The authorities in Petrograd were not unprepared for disorders in the streets. During January and February Minister of the Interior, Protopopov, had brought in additional police and reinforced the garrison of the city with, what were believed to be, reliable troops. All revolutionaries still at large, such as the Petrograd committee of the Bolsheviks, and the Menshevik members of the War Industries Committee, were arrested. But such measures were to prove of little use, for the revolution, when it came, owed little to the professional revolutionaries, many of whom were either living abroad or in exile in Siberia. The movement which overthrew the Russian monarchy was 'leaderless, spontaneous and anonymous'.

Reasons for Unrest

1 Lack of food and fuel caused by transport difficulties and the reluctance of the peasants to sell their produce to the towns.
2 The failure of wages to keep pace with the increase in prices.
3 The repressive attitude of government towards labour organizations.
4 The hardships brought by the war, the continual military defeats and the effects of anti-war propaganda.
5 The feeling of shared suffering among the 400,000 industrial workers of Petrograd, who tended to be concentrated in a few large factories.

This poster calls for 'Help for the starving'

63

Distribution of revolutionary propaganda leaflets

Timetable of a Revolution

February 25 crowds of up to 500 marched through the streets of Petrograd, broke shop windows, shouted anti-war slogans.

February 26 similar scenes repeated on Nevsky Prospect – some Bolshevik slogans.

March 7 the management of the giant Putilov works refused workers' demands for higher wages and declared a lock-out, thereby putting out onto the streets of Petrograd, 20,000 of the most politically conscious, and revolutionary workers in Russia.

March 8 The Tsar left Petrograd for Army Headquarters at Mogilev. Demonstrations, in celebration of International Womens' Day, took place and developed into demands for bread. As a result of strikes about fifty factories were closed and 90,000 workers were out on the streets. Cossacks and police were sent out to disperse the crowds and by the end of the day the authorities seemed to have the situation under control.

March 9 There were now some 200,000 workers on strike. The marches and demonstrations now moved, from the working class district of Vyborg, over the river to the centre of the city. Attacks on

the police took place, with the crowd using cobble-stones, lumps of ice and sticks. Cossacks were sent out to disperse the crowds gathering on the Nevsky Prospect, but instead they mixed freely with the demonstrators.

March 10 The strike became general. Students joined the demonstrators. Clashes with the police increased. The Cossacks again displayed reluctance to disperse the crowds, who tried to avoid provoking the troops.

The Tsaritsa wrote to Nicholas:

'This is a hooligan movement, young people run and shout that there is no bread, simply to create excitement, along with workers who prevent others from working. If the weather were very cold they would all probably stay at home. But all this will pass and become calm, if only the Duma will behave itself.'

The Tsar sent a telegram to General Khabalov, Commander of the Petrograd garrison:

'I command you to suppress from tomorrow all disorders on the streets of the capital, which are

(top left) Petrograd demonstration. The banner reads 'Stand together to protect our freedom'.
(top right) Armed 'militia' of workers and soldiers. (above) Cossacks join the demonstrators. The banner reads 'Down with the Monarchy. Long live the Republic'.

impermissable at a time when the fatherland is carrying on a difficult war with Germany.'

Khabalov then issued instructions to fire on the crowds if they refused to disperse after warnings.

March 11 Troops fired on demonstrators in different parts of the city – around eighty people were killed or wounded. Some soldiers of the Pavlovsk regiment mutinied but the rebellion was quickly put down. The government issued an order to dissolve the Duma. Rodzianko, the President of the Duma, sent a telegram to the Tsar:

> 'The situation is serious. There is anarchy in the capital. The government is paralysed. It is necessary immediately to entrust a person who enjoys the confidence of the country with the formation of a new government. There must be no delay. Hesitation is fatal.'

March 12 The decisive day; several regiments mutinied and joined the demonstrators, thus ensuring the success of the revolution. They proceeded to the Vyborg district where they broke into arsenals, armed the workers and joined with them in hunting down the police. General Khabalov ordered the rest of his troops to suppress the disorders, but they refused to obey orders and joined the crowds in the streets. The city passed completely into the hands of the revolutionaries. An eye-witness described the scene:

> 'Incessant firing reached my ears . . . Groups of citizens huddled against walls of houses to avoid flying bullets. On the Liteinyi blazed a very fierce fire, the magnificent building of the High Court being in flames . . . other government buildings were also burning, among them police stations. . . . On the faces of many spectators of this destruction were expressions of intense

The funeral of a victim of the revolution: The banner reads 'You fell as a sacrifice'.

satisfaction. Their countenances, in the red blaze, looked demoniac as they shouted, laughed and danced. Here and there were heaped wooden carvings of the Russian double eagle, torn from shops and Government Buildings, which were being thrown on the fires, to the cheers of the crowd. The old regime was disappearing in the ashes and no one regretted them.'

The Formation of the Provisional Government The workers had overthrown the Romanov dynasty, but they had nothing with which to replaced it. Attention now turned to the Duma as the only national, representative organization still in existence. The Duma, however, did not know what to do. Rodzianko said: 'I am no revolutionary. . . . But there is no government any longer. Everything falls to me . . .' He decided to send another telegram to the Tsar:

> 'The situation is growing worse. Measures should be taken immediately as tomorrow will be

Michael Rodzianko, President of the Duma.

too late. The last hour has struck when the fate of the country and the dynasty is being decided.'

The Tsar did not respond to the appeal:

'Again that fat-bellied Rodzianko has written me a lot of nonsense which I won't even bother to answer.'

The Duma decided not to disperse as ordered but continued to meet in an unofficial fashion, besieged by the crowds outside demanding action. Rodzianko made a last effort to get the Tsar to concede a responsible ministry headed either by himself or the *Zemstvo* leader, Prince Lvov. The Tsar refused. Meanwhile, in another part of the Tauride Palace, groups of workers and soldiers had set up a Soviet of Workers' and Soldiers' Deputies. The Duma had to take action or be destroyed by a movement it was unable to control. As one member put it: 'If we don't take power, others will take it, those who have already elected some scoundrels in the factories.'

A provisional committee of the Duma was set up which on 14 March nominated a Provisional Government with Prince George Lvov as prime minister.

The Abdication of the Tsar Nicholas II left Mogilev early on 13 March for Tsarskoye Selo, but his train was diverted to General Ruzsky's headquarters at Pskov when it was learned that revolutionaries controlled the railways into Petrograd. Having no information concerning the rapid developments in Petrograd the Tsar decided, on 14 March, that he would permit Rodzianko to head a ministry responsible to the Duma. This decision came too late. On 15 March the Tsar was informed, by all the leading generals of the army, that only his abdication could save the Monarchy and preserve discipline in the army sufficient to continue fighting the war. Nicholas at first agreed to abdicate in favour of his son but, after discussions with the boy's doctor, who told him that the Tsarevich's haemophilia was incurable, he issued a manifesto which stated in part:

'During these days, which are decisive for Russia, we have deemed it to be our duty to help our people to draw close together so as to attain victory as soon as possible. Thus, in agreement with the State Duma we have judged it right to abdicate the throne of the Russian State, and to lay down the supreme power.

As we do not wish to separate from our beloved son, we have transferred our inheritance to our brother, Grand Duke Michael Alexandrovich. . . .'

On 16 March the Duma Committee offered the crown to the Grand Duke who decided that, under the circumstances, he could not accept the throne. Russia became a Republic and on 21 March the Royal Family were placed under house arrest at Tsarskoye Selo. Three centuries of absolute rule by the Romanovs had come to an end – not as a result of a carefully organized plot or a planned seizure of power, but as a consequence of a spontaneous, unorganized popular movement. So weak and

Ex-Tsar Nicholas at Tsarskoye Selo

4 What evidence can you find to support the view that the Duma only took action with great reluctance?
5 What factors persuaded the Tsar of the need to abdicate?

The Provisional Government

The new government was largely composed of Kadets and the moderately conservative Octobrists. The leading figures in the new cabinet were the Minister of Foreign Affairs, Paul Milyukov; the Minister of War, Guchkov and the Minister of Justice, the Socialist Revolutionary, Alexander Kerensky.

This government had taken on the responsibility of ruling Russia, but it totally lacked the power to do so. It was supported only by the tiny educated minority of the population. Among the city workers and the peasant masses it aroused little enthusiasm. They, like the soldiers, preferred to give their loyalty to the Soviet of Workers' and Soldiers' Deputies.

The Petrograd Soviet While the Duma had been dithering about taking power, in Room 13 of that same Tauride Palace a Soviet had been set up. It was this body of soldiers and workers which took over the running of, the now paralysed, Petrograd. They re-opened the banks, ran the trains and organized food supplies. By April 1917 Russia was covered by a network of Soviets based on the Petrograd model, which was itself a revival of the organization created in 1905. The Petrograd Soviet was a body of some 1500 deputies, who were elected on the basis of one man per thousand factory workers and one soldier per company, and who were subject to instant recall. Its political leadership was provided by Menshevik and Social-

discredited had the regime become that there was no section of Russian society prepared to fight for its preservation.

Assignment

1 What steps had the government taken to prevent disorders in Petrograd?
2 Why did the workers of Petrograd take to the streets?
3 What was the main reason for the success of the demonstrators in overthrowing the government?

ist Revolutionary activists, its mass support by the more numerous soldiers. It was they who were responsible for the issue of a proclamation (Order No. 1) to the Petrograd garrison which stated:

1 'In all companies, battalions, regiments, committees from the elected representatives of the lower ranks shall be chosen immediately.
2 In all those military units which have not yet chosen their representatives to the Soviet of Workers' Deputies, one representative from each company shall be selected.
3 In all its political actions, the military branch is subordinated to the Soviet of Workers' and Soldiers' Deputies and to its own committees.
4 The orders of the military commission of the State Duma shall be executed only in such cases as do not conflict with the orders and resolutions of the Soviet.
5 All kinds of arms, must be kept at the disposal and under the control of the company and battalion committees, and in no case be turned over to officers even at their demand.
6 Standing at attention and compulsory saluting, when not on duty is abolished.'

This instruction was taken up by the whole Russian army and contributed to its speedy disintegration. It also served to weaken from the outset the authority of the Provisional Government, whose complete helplessness was expressed by Minister of War, Guchkov, to the Commander-in-Chief, General Alekseev:

'The Provisional Government possesses no real power and its orders are executed only in so far as this is permitted by the Soviet of Workers' and Soldiers' Deputies, which holds in its hands the most important elements of actual power, such as troops, railroads, postal and telegraph services. It is possible to say directly that the Provisional Government exists only while this is permitted by the Soviet.'

A Provisional Government poster urges 'War until Victory'.

Early Successes For the first two months after the March Revolution the Provisional Government and the Petrograd Soviet co-existed in an uneasy alliance and were responsible for a number of reforms:

1 An 8-hour day was introduced into many industries. Trade unions were made legal.
2 Political prisoners were released from prison or exile.

3 Capital punishment and exile to Siberia were abolished.
4 Trial by jury was introduced and independent judges appointed.
5 Poland was given independence and autonomy was granted to Finland.
6 Discrimination against religious and racial minorities was made illegal.
7 Freedom of speech and of the press was introduced. Censorship was abolished.
8 A Constituent Assembly was to be held, whose members, chosen by secret ballot of all the people, were to establish the new constitution for the country.

However desirable each of these measures were, they did nothing to resolve the major difficulties which engulfed Russia at this time. The government's failure to deal with the problems of land for the peasants, peace for the soldiers, food for the towns, and control of industry for the workers, was to be exploited to the full with the return to Petrograd of the Bolshevik leader, Lenin.

The Return of Lenin

The Sealed Train Lenin was in Switzerland when he first received news of the overthrow of the Tsar. He was anxious to return to Russia as soon as possible, but he faced certain difficulties. The Allies controlled all the possible routes out of Switzerland and into Russia, and they were unlikely to help a notorious revolutionary whose anti-war views were well known. At this point the German authorities were made aware of Lenin's quandary by a former revolutionary associate known as Parvus. The Germans were anxious to foment as much disorder as possible inside Russia, in order to weaken the new government and oblige it to sign a separate peace, thus releasing German troops for the war in the west. They agreed to

Lenin's return to Russia, April 1917

provide the Bolshevik leader with funds and a passage through Germany. The negotiations were handled by a Swiss Socialist, Fritz Platten, who secured the sealed train which was to transport Lenin, and some thirty other revolutionary exiles, to the Baltic coast where they would take ship for Sweden. The German military authorities permitted the transit of this train through Germany only on the condition that none of its passengers be allowed out, lest they spread their dangerous revolutionary theories among the German populace. Lenin left Switzerland on 9 April and, travelling via Finland, reached Petrograd on 16 April.

Lenin is welcomed on his return

At the Finland Station Lenin's arrival in Petrograd was greeted by a guard of honour, an official reception, bouquets, cheering crowds and formal speeches. Chkheidze, the Menshevik chairman of the Petrograd Soviet, welcomed the returning revolutionary with a cautionary message.

'Comrade Lenin, in the name of the Petrograd Soviet we welcome you to Russia. But we think that the main task . . . is now the defence of the Revolution against any attacks on it, whether from within or without. We consider that what this goal requires is not disunion, but the closing of the ranks. We hope you will pursue these goals together with us.'

Lenin's reply was polite but uncompromising. The March Revolution must only be the beginning:

'I am happy to greet you – you the victorious Russian Revolution. . . . The robbers' imperialist war is the beginning of civil war in all Europe . . . Long live the world-wide socialist revolution.'

The 'April Theses' The Bolsheviks had played little part in the events leading to the March Revolution and had had little influence on the developments which had come after it. Lenin was determined that Party policy should have both direction and consistency, and that required driving, uncompromising leadership.

On his first night he addressed the Party leadership at their temporary headquarters, the villa of the ballerina Kshessinskaya. The following day he spoke to a general meeting of social democrats of all persuasions. On both occasions his listeners were stunned. The reception was hostile. He was accused of anarchism, indeed of madness. What had he said to arouse such a response? His arguments were contained in the *April Theses*:

1 The Provisional Government should not be supported. It was necessary to work for a second revolution in which power would pass to the Soviets.

2 Anti-war propaganda should be carried on in the army. The soldiers should be encouraged to fraternize with the Germans. Only with the overthrow of capitalism could the war be brought to an end.

3 Capitalism in Russia must be wiped out. The factories should be given over into the control of the workers.

4 The land of Russia should be nationalized. All estates should be confiscated and divided up by peasant soviets.

Kamenev and other leading Bolsheviks argued that it was unrealistic to call for a socialist revolution at this time, and complained that Lenin's policy would isolate the Bolsheviks from all other left-wing parties. But by the end of April Lenin had overcome the opposition within the Party and, as one historian has said, the Party members 'found themselves committed to a war on the Provisional Government and its foreign policy, to capturing the Soviets from the Mensheviks and Socialist Revolutionaries as a means of seizing state power, and to encouraging the peasants to take land in an organized way.'

Russian Imperialism by 1917

Assignment

1 What weaknesses beset the Provisional Government from the beginning?

2 For what reasons would Soviet Order No. 1 hasten the disintegration of the Russian Army and weaken the authority of the Provisional Government?

3 Outline the successes and failures of the Provisional Government.

4 Why do you think the Germans were prepared to help Lenin return to Russia?

5 In your own words, outline Lenin's *April Theses*.

Chapter Nine

War and counter-revolution

The War Aims Crisis

On 9 April the Petrograd Soviet had issued an appeal for peace:

'We are appealing to our brother proletarians of the Austro-German coalition. The Russian Revolution will not retreat before the bayonets of conquerors and will not allow itself to be crushed by military force. But we are calling to you, throw off the yoke of your semi-autocratic rule as the Russian people have shaken off the Tsar's – and then by our united efforts we will stop the horrible butchery which is disgracing humanity and is beclouding the great days of the birth of Russian freedom. Proletarians of all Countries, unite.'

The formula of the Soviet was a peace without annexations and indemnities – sometimes known as revolutionary defencism.

On 1 May Milyukov, Foreign Minister in the Provisional Government, sent this document to the Allies but added an accompanying note which spoke of 'war to the victorious end', and of the government's intention to keep its promises to the Allies and observe the secret treaties, as well as supporting such guarantees and sanctions required to prevent new bloody encounters in the future.

When this became public on 3 May there was an immediate storm of protest. The streets filled with armed soldiers and demonstrators and clashes between rival groups continued for two days. There were demands for Milyukov's resignation and the Provisional Government was obliged to issue an explanation of Milyukov's note which was then sent to the Allied ambassadors:

'Free Russia does not aim at the domination of other nations, or at occupying by force foreign territories. Its aim is not to subjugate or humiliate anyone. In referring to the "penalties and guarantees" essential to a durable peace the Provisional Government had in view reduction of armaments, the establishment of international tribunals etc.'

This statement satisfied the Soviet but not the Bolsheviks who were able to portray the Provisional Government as bound hand and foot to the English and French bankers, and to urge that it give way to the Soviets. The crisis did lead to a reorganization of the government. Milyukov and Guchkov, the Minister of War, resigned and six socialist members of the Soviet entered the government. The new Minister of War, Alexander Kerensky, was the dominant figure in the new Cabinet.

The Morale of the Army By the spring of 1917 the fighting capabilities of the Russian Army had been seriously weakened. Not only was it no longer a force capable of mounting an offensive, it was unable even to offer serious resistance to the German and Austrian armies. The effect of the Petrograd Soviet's Order No. 1, and the Subse-

Army morale: soldiers at the front welcome the revolution (top); soldiers reading Bolshevik propaganda. (above)

quent Declaration of the Rights of Soldiers, had been to take away the control of the troops from the officers and give it into the hands of elected soldiers' committees. Officers were frequently dismissed by their men, arrested and sometimes shot. The commanders quickly despaired of the situation. At the end of March General Dragomirov complained that: 'All the thoughts of the common soldiers turn towards home. Their only desire is to leave the trenches.'

Desertions rapidly increased after March 1917. By the end of October some two million men had unofficially left the army. Demoralization grew with each passing month. The ordinary soldier was not inclined to fight and, perhaps to die, for a policy which talked of a 'peace without annexations and indemnities'. Whole armies refused to move to the front line. German peace propaganda and Bolshevik papers enjoyed an increasing readership among the soldiers.

It was with these soldiers that Kerensky, in response to demands from the Allies, agreed to attack the Austrians through Galicia in July 1917.

Alexander Kerensky

Kerensky was the leading figure in the Cabinet, and was to be the dominant personality in what remained of the life of the Provisional Government. This young lawyer of thirty-five was a Socialist Revolutionary, a former deputy of the old Duma and a Vice-President of the Petrograd Soviet. He was a flamboyant speaker with a sense of the theatrical, capable of rousing the masses. Kerensky believed it was possible to restore the discipline and fighting spirit of the army and embarked on a speechmaking tour of the front line to rally the troops.

He appointed a new Commander-in-Chief, Brusilov, in place of the ailing Alekseev and provided the troops with immense quantities of artillery and munitions.

The July Offensive The Russian offensive began on 1 July. Superiority in guns and men combined with the war weariness and poor morale of the Austrians enabled the Russians to make early advances and take many prisoners. But the attack petered out within two weeks – many troops refused to enter the front line, others refused to obey orders to advance and consolidate the early Russian successes. On 19 July German troops counter-attacked and turned the Russian advance into a disastrous rout. Thousands of Russians deserted. Thousands more abandoned themselves in an orgy of burning, outrage and pillage. Galicia was lost. The Russian army suffered a complete military collapse – as a fighting machine it was 'irretrievably ruined'.

Assignment

1 What were the causes of the War Aims crisis?
2 What grounds are there for the view that the Russian Army 'was no longer a force capable of mounting an offensive'?
3 What reasons can you put forward for the decline in morale of the Russian Army?
4 What steps did Kerensky take to prepare the Army for the July Offensive?
5 What evidence is there to show that the Russian Army 'as a fighting machine was irretrievably ruined'?

The Russian Offensive, July 1917.

The Deepening of the Revolution

The period from March to July 1917 witnessed a move to the Left inside Russia – a deepening of the Revolution. The workers and soldiers displayed an increasing contempt and disregard for, not only the Provisional Government, but also the Petrograd Soviet itself. In the countryside peasants seized land; in the towns workers confiscated houses. In the Army soldiers disregarded their officers.

Growing Unrest In Finland and the Ukraine there were increasing demands for self-government, and in many provinces local Soviets declared their independence from the Provisional Government.

In the factories, wage demands and agitation for workers' control led to a steady increase in strikes and a steady decline in industrial output. By June 1917 the industrial workers had gone over to the Bolsheviks in increasing numbers, sending them as factory delegates to the Soviets.

In the countryside, there was mounting unrest. The Government wished to postpone the redivision of estates until after the election of a Constituent Assembly. Many leading Kadets wished to defer both until after the end of the war. They argued that to give out land at this point would destroy the Army. But when news of illegal land seizures reached the soldiers they deserted anyway. At this time the peasants continued to support the Socialist Revolutionaries; the Bolsheviks had little influence in the countryside but their strength was growing elsewhere.

Growth of Bolshevik Support In February 1917 the Party had numbered 20,000; by April it had grown to 80,000 and by August it was to reach 200,000. In mid-May Trotsky returned to Russia from the U.S.A. and, although previously an opponent of the Bolsheviks, he quickly joined the Party and played a vital role as speech-maker and personality in the Soviet. Despite this growth in support the Bolsheviks were still very much a

A Bolshevik addresses the crowds in Petrograd. May Day 1917

minority group. In June the first All-Russian Congress of Soviets was held and of the 822 voting delegates the Bolsheviks could muster only 105. This did not prevent Lenin from openly stating – 'The Bolshevik Party is ready at any moment to assume full power. . . . The War can only be ended by further development of the Revolution.'

The Bolsheviks attempted to display their growing strength by calling for a demonstration of support on the streets of Petrograd on 22 June. For once the Soviet asserted itself and banned the demonstration. The Bolsheviks backed down but were able to turn a demonstration on 1 July, called by the Soviet, into a display of popular support for Lenin and his Party. The Bolshevik slogans – 'All Power to the Soviets', 'Bread, Peace and Freedom' – were much in evidence. Despite this success the dangers of street politics were to be quickly brought home to the Bolsheviks with the disturbances of 16–17 July.

The July Days Unrest had been growing in the capital from early July. Food shortages and price rises had provoked wage demands, and strikes had subsequently taken place at a number of factories including the militant Putilov works. Older soldiers, who had been given leave to return home for the spring sowing, were recalled to the colours for the July offensive, and had demonstrated their opposition to the war in Petrograd and other towns. The First Machine-Gun Regiment decided to send to the front only ten of the thirty detachments requested by the military authorities, and threatened the Provisional Government with extinction should it, or the Soviet, attempt action against the regiment. All these incidents created a highly-charged atmosphere in the capital, which was sparked off on 15 July with the resignation of four Kadet Ministers from the Cabinet.

The workers and soldiers took advantage of this government crisis to come out onto the streets under the slogan 'All Power to the Soviets'. This created problems for the Bolsheviks who were not prepared for a seizure of power at this time but could not afford to allow the revolutionary movement to slip away into the hands of more extreme groups. They therefore supported the demonstration while attempting to restrain and control it; but huge numbers of armed soldiers, supported by 20,000 Kronstadt sailors, and groups of workers from every major factory in the city, came out. Much indiscriminate shooting took place.

After three days of confusion and bloodshed the demonstrators, lacking leadership, returned to their homes and barracks. Although the Provisional Government could have been easily overthrown the Soviet refused to take power and denounced those soldiers and workers who had invaded the Tauride Palace.

July Days in Petrograd: armed workers and students

July Days in Petrograd: bloodshed and confusion (above); Lenin in disguise (below) used this passport photo to escape to Finland.

July Days and the Bolsheviks The July Days could have led to the destruction of the Bolsheviks as an effective political force inside Russia. They had associated themselves with a movement which seemed to be demanding an armed revolt, and were thus liable to the consequences of defeat once it failed. On the 18 July the Government published a set of documents, some of which were forged, which seemed to show that Lenin was a German agent, spending German gold to undermine the Provisional Government and bring about a separate peace. This information, which contained some truth, turned popular support away from the Bolsheviks and enabled action to be taken against them. The offices and printing shop of the Bolshevik paper, *Pravda*, were wrecked; party members were driven out of Kshessinskaya's villa; Kamenev, Trotsky and other leading Bolsheviks were arrested; Lenin and Zinoviev fled in disguise to Finland. The Bolsheviks were labelled traitors to

the Revolution and hostility to the Party spread through vast areas of the country.

The Kornilov Revolt

On 21 July Prince Lvov resigned and Kerensky became Prime Minister. His new cabinet was more conservative than its predecessor and was determined to halt the slide towards chaos. It quickly banned street meetings and demonstrations; it disbanded some of the more revolutionary regiments and restored the death penalty at the front; it restricted the press and condemned land seizures by the peasants; it seized weapons from civilians and postponed further the calling of a Constituent Assembly.

But these measures did not go far enough for many army officers, industrialists, land-owners and others, who regarded Kerensky as too weak, and too much under the influence of the Soviet. They placed their hopes for the salvation of Russia in the appearance of a military strong man, and believed that they had found him in the new Commander-in-Chief, General Lavr Kornilov.

Kornilov, the son of a poor Siberian Cossack, had had a distinguished military career and had frequently distinguished himself in acts of personal courage. He had accepted the supreme command on 16 July only on condition that he could enforce strict discipline on the army by field court-martial and executions, and that such measures must be extended to those areas in the rear where reserves were stationed. His solution to Russia's problems was simple:

> 'The time has come to hang the German agents and spies headed by Lenin and to disperse the Soviet of Workers' and Soldiers' Deputies so that it can never reassemble.'

Kerensky was prepared to use Kornilov to

Kerensky as Prime Minister, uses the ex-Tsar's study in the Winter Palace (top) Kornilov as Commander-in-Chief, tried to counteract Bolshevik propaganda in the army (above)

destroy the Bolsheviks and intimidate the Soviet, but Kornilov, unable to distinguish between the moderate socialism of Kerensky and the more extreme Leninist variety, decided to overthrow the prime minister and set himself up as a military dictator. Kerensky dismissed him from his post on 9 September. Kornilov refused to resign and sent his troops against Petrograd.

The Defeat of Kornilov Kerensky denounced Kornilov and demanded his arrest. He then called upon the Soviets and the people of Petrograd to repulse the advancing Cossacks of General Krymov, whom Kornilov had sent against the city. This was a fateful decision for both Kornilov and Kerensky, as the Soviet set up a Committee for Struggle with Counter-Revolution which the Bolsheviks were invited to join. Lenin saw the opportunity to restore the prestige the Party had lost during the July Days and at the same time discredit Kerensky: 'We will fight with Kornilov, but we will not support Kerensky.'

The Bolsheviks successfully urged the creation of an armed workers militia, which brought about the legalization and re-arming of the Bolshevik Red Guards, who had been suppressed after the July disturbances. Some 25,000 recruits were enlisted, armed with both rifles and machine-guns, while others were mobilized by the Bolsheviks for trench digging and fortifying Petrograd. As Trotsky later claimed: 'The army that rose against Kornilov was the army-to-be of the October Revolution.'

Kornilov's soldiers were never to reach the revolutionary capital. The railway workers did their duty. Regiments would arrive in the wrong division. All the big stations had their own Soviets, the telegraphers kept them informed of all movements and also held up Kornilov's orders. From the direction of Petrograd innumerable delegations continued to arrive from regiments sent out to oppose the Kornilovists. Before fighting they wanted to talk things over. Meetings were continuous and at them all, the cry was being raised 'They have deceived us'. The revolt petered out in near farce. General Krymov shot himself rather than face charges of mutiny.

The successful defence of the Revolution brought no glory to Kerensky. The army officers who had supported Kornilov felt that Kerensky had deceived their leaders and were unlikely to come to the aid of either himself or his government if it were threatened in the future, while on the Left, it has been said, by the writer L. Kochan, that:

'The part taken by the Bolsheviks in the struggle against Kornilov helped to turn them, in popular eyes, from traitors to the revolution into its most ardent defenders.'

Assignment

1 What examples can you give to illustrate the growing unrest within Russia between March and July 1917?
2 Why was the government reluctant to tackle the land problem at this time?
3 Why did the activities of the militant workers and soldiers create problems for the Bolsheviks at this time?
4 What action did the government take against the Bolsheviks?
5 What steps did the new government of Kerensky take to halt Russia's slide into chaos?
6 What steps did the Petrograd Soviet take to defend the city against Kornilov's troops?

Chapter Ten

The road to the Winter Palace

Background

Kerenksy had survived the threat posed by Kornilov but his government was becoming increasingly isolated politically. On the Right, the propertied classes who had supported Kornilov were sullen in their defeat and resentful of Kerensky's double dealing, while on the Left, the soldiers and industrial workers were turning towards the Bolsheviks and their allies. By the autumn of 1917 the Provisional Government was quickly losing what remained of its already limited authority.

In the end the Provisional Government fell because it failed to:
1 End an increasingly unpopular war
2 Transfer the land speedily to the peasants
3 Improve the supply of food to the towns
4 Prevent the collapse of industrial production.

The Breakdown of the Russian Army The crushing defeats suffered in Galicia during July speeded up the collapse of the Russian Army. At the front there were shortages of food, footwear and clothing. The rate of desertion increased daily. Everywhere the desire was for peace and land – a hope fostered by Bolshevik papers such as *Soldiers Truth* and *Trench Truth*.

The Kornilov revolt destroyed what little trust the soldiers retained in their superiors. Officers went in fear for their lives. The Government, however, had no intention of ending the war. They would stay loyal to their allies in the west and wage war to a victorious conclusion.

The Peasant Uprising During the summer of 1917 peasant communities had been formed in the countryside which removed the land-owners and disposed of privately owned meadows, woods and pastures. From September onwards the pace of land seizures and destruction of estates accelerated. They also became much more violent, partly as a

Russian army banners: 'Proletarians of all countries unite!' 'Long-live the Democratic Republic.'

result of more and more soldiers deserting from the army and returning to their native villages. Manor houses were looted, their buildings burned to the ground; the owners and employees were driven out, frequently beaten, often murdered.

The government of Kerensky issued futile warnings against peasant disorders and insisted that land reforms await the Constituent Assembly.

The Revolt of the Workers The Provisional Government had done little to halt the decline in living standards of the city workers. Moscow suffered shortages of bread, meat, potatoes and grain during the spring and summer. By autumn Petrograd was short of bread, milk, sugar and tobacco. Street robberies and housebreakings increased. Food riots and the looting of shops were reported from numerous cities throughout Russia. Such food as was available rose rapidly in price, quickly outstripping wage rises.

Trade Unions, which had flourished after the overthrow of the Tsar, were unable to satisfy the demands of the workers who increasingly looked to their elected factory committees for leadership. By June the factory committees were dominated by the Bolsheviks and had adopted a programme of workers' control. Owners and managers were driven out of the factories, sometimes assaulted, occasionally killed. Employers responded to the take over of their factories with lock-outs and plant closures. Unemployment increased: productivity and profits declined. The workers, in retaliation, waged increasingly bitter strikes.

The response of the Provisional Government was to issue decrees which insisted that: 'The task of every worker before the country and the revolution is to devote all his strength to intensive labour and not lose a minute of working time.'

The support of the industrial workers was to be crucial for the Bolsheviks, for it provided them with the mass support necessary to carry out the Revolution for which they had begun to prepare.

Assignment

1 What evidence is there that by the autumn of 1917 the Provisional Government had lost control of events inside Russia?
2 For what reasons did the Provisional Government lose the support of the majority of Russians?
3 Is it true to say that the Russian Army had collapsed by late 1917? Give reasons for your answer.
4 What evidence is there that the peasants were not prepared to wait on legal land reforms?
5 Describe conditions in the cities and towns of Russia in late 1917.
6 What reasons can you suggest for the increasing industrial unrest at this time?

Bolshevik Strength

Throughout the autumn of 1917 popular support for the Bolsheviks increased. In September the Bolsheviks obtained a majority in the Petrograd Soviet and Trotsky, released from prison to help deal with Kornilov, became the President. The same pattern was repeated in Moscow, Kiev and other industrial cities. Bolshevik strength lay in Petrograd, the Moscow industrial area, the Ural towns, in Finland and among the soldiers of the northern front and the sailors of the Baltic Fleet based at Kronstadt. At no time did they gain the support of the majority of the population however, for the peasant masses, the vast bulk of the population, continued to support the loosely knit Socialist Revolutionary groups.

Lenin talking to workers in 1917.

Lenin's Decision A second Revolution was not inevitable in Russia in 1917. The decision to stage an armed uprising was made by one man, as W.H. Chamberlin has written:

'Lenin's indisputable claim to greatness as a revolutionary leader lies in the fact that he realized immediately after the collapse of Kornilov that the time for action had come, that he drove home this view . . . and that he never relaxed his pressure on the Party Central Committee . . . until the opposition was crushed and the Party organization had swung into line behind his proposals.'

The opposition to the seizure of power was led by Zinoviev and Kamenev who wanted to wait and count on a Bolshevik victory in the Constituent Assembly. They feared for the Party, the Revolution and for Russia, should such a gamble as proposed by Lenin fail. The arguments continued during September and into October, not merely within the Party but (somewhat surprisingly) also in the left-wing press. Lenin returned from Finland and held a meeting of the Central Committee on 23 October.

The writer, A.B. Ulam, describes what then took place:

'Once again he went through and refuted the possible objections to an immediate uprising. No point in waiting or talking. Time to begin. The others were sceptical . . . But finally the will of one man prevailed. By ten to two, with Zinoviev and Kamenev voting against the motion, the Committee called for an armed uprising.'

Trotsky's Action The decision to stage an uprising taken, Lenin returned to hiding. The planning of the insurrection fell to Trotsky, who decided that it should be timed to coincide with the meeting of the second All-Russian Congress of Soviets. The Bolsheviks had to appear to be defending the rights of the Soviets not simply to be seizing power for themselves. The instrument of revolt was to be the Military Revolutionary Committee of the Soviet, which had been suggested by the Mensheviks but was now dominated by the Bolsheviks and their Left Socialist Revolutionary allies. As the writer Ulam explains, Trotsky seemed to be everywhere:

'issuing orders to the Military Revolutionary Committee, presiding over the Soviet, addressing the soldiers' and workers' meetings. His flamboyance and theatricality, which were to earn so many enemies in sober everyday politics,

Trotsky, organizer of the Revolution, with Sverdlov on his left, 1917.

now served him well when people had to be infused with a sense of daring and the romance of action.'

His task was to demoralize and weaken those elements who supported the Provisional Government and to stir up the pro-Bolshevik forces to a pitch of excitement and a conviction in the rightness of their cause.

'The Soviet regime will give everything that is in the country to the poor and to the people in the trenches. You, boorzhui, have two coats – hand over one to the soldier who is cold in the trenches. You have warm boots? Sit at home; the worker needs your boots. Who will stand for the cause of the workers and peasants to the last drop of blood?'

Trotsky concluded; and the throng of thousands, as if hypnotized, all raised their hands.

'Let this voting of yours be your vow, with all your strength, at any sacrifice, to support the Soviet, which has taken on itself the great task of bringing the victory of the Revolution to the end, and of giving land, bread and peace.'

On the Eve The Bolsheviks had set up their headquarters in the Smolny Institute, a former girls' convent school, which already housed the Petrograd Soviet and the Military Revolutionary Committee. An eye-witness describes the scene:

'The long, vaulted corridors, lit by rare electric lights, were thronged with hurrying shapes of soldiers and workmen, some bent under the weight of huge bundles of newspapers, proclamations, printed propaganda of all sorts.'

It was no secret that the Bolsheviks were planning to seize power but the Provisional Government took few precautions against it. Kerensky seemed to welcome the opportunity of destroying the Bolsheviks once and for all. Meanwhile,

'In the factories the committee-rooms were filled with stacks of rifles, couriers came and went, the Red Guard drilled. . . . In all the barracks meetings every night, and all day long interminable hot arguments.'

Red Guards in front of the Smolny Institute

Finally, on 4 November the Government took action. Relations were broken off with the Military Revolutionary Committee and the arrest of the members ordered. The next day Kerensky closed down all the Bolshevik newspapers and cut off the telephones to the Smolny Institute. He then summoned loyal troops – mainly officer-cadets (Junkers) and Cossacks – to occupy the important buildings in the city and to patrol the streets. Petrograd, Kerensky declared, was in a state of insurrection.

Hanging by a Thread On the night of 6 November Lenin emerged from hiding, made his way to Bolshevik headquarters at Smolny and issued the following instructions:

'I am writing these lines on the evening of November 6th. The situation is critical in the extreme. It is absolutely clear that to delay the insurrection now will be inevitably fatal.

I exhort my comrades with all my heart and strength to realize that everything now hangs by a thread, that we are being confronted by problems that cannot be solved by conferences and congresses (even Congresses of Soviets) but exclusively by the people, the masses, by the struggle of the armed masses.

We must at all costs, this very evening, this very night, arrest the Government, first disarming the Junkers and so forth. We must not wait! We may lose everything! History will not forgive revolutionaries for procrastinating when they can be victorious today, while they risk losing much, in fact, everything, tomorrow!'

During the night of the 6th and the early morning of the 7th the forces of the Military Revolutionary Committee occupied all the strategic points in the city – the railway stations, the telephone exchange and the State Bank. The cruiser *Aurora* anchored near the Nicholai Bridge, and some torpedo boats entered the Neva. Almost everywhere the officer-cadets and Cossacks gave up their positions without resistance. There was virtually no bloodshed and a minimum of looting and

Lenin at the Smolny, among the dustcovers of Tsarism

Red Guards take over the telephone exchange

The Winter Palace, seen from the River Neva.

disorder. Throughout the day government buildings were surrounded by Red Guards then occupied. Only the Winter Palace, seat of the Provisional Government, remained to be taken.

The 'Storming' of the Winter Palace

The delay in attacking the Palace was caused by the refusal of the gunners of the Peter and Paul Fortress to bombard it, on the grounds that the cannon were in a state of disrepair, and that it would be dangerous to have them fired. The attackers were obliged to await the arrival of naval gunners from Kronstadt. The Winter Palace was defended by Cossacks, officer-cadets and a Women's Battalion, but by the early evening many of these had slipped quietly away. About 9 p.m. a blank shell was fired from the *Aurora* which provoked a heated exchange of rifle and machine-gun fire from both sides. At 10 p.m. the Women's Battalion was captured and disarmed. At 11 p.m. the guns from Peter and Paul opened up but inflicted little damage. The attackers, now reinforced, had entered the Palace, and numerous scuffles and minor clashes took place in the maze of corridors and galleries which interlaced the huge building. Outside, a group from Petrograd City Council and other leading anti-Bolsheviks

arrived to show their support for the ministers besieged inside. They were dispersed peacefully by the sailors guarding the way across the Nevsky. At last, the invaders, led by Antonov and Chudnovsky reached the corridor leading to the inner room in which the Government ministers had sought their final refuge.

The doors were burst open, the room was filled with armed men, led by Antonov who shouted: 'I declare to you, members of the Provisional Govern-

Storming the Winter Palace, 7 November 1917

ment, that you are under arrest. I am a member of the Military Revolutionary Committee.'

'The members of the Provisional Government submit to violence and surrender, in order to avoid bloodshed,' replied Konovalov.

The arrested ministers were escorted across the Neva to the fortress of Peter and Paul and consigned to the dungeons. The struggle for the Winter Palace had been won.

The Bolsheviks Assume Power On the morning of 7 November when the struggle for the Winter Palace had not yet begun the Bolsheviks announced, somewhat prematurely that:

'The Provisional Government has been overthrown. State power has passed into the hands of the Military Revolutionary Committee. The cause for which the people have fought; the immediate proposal of a democratic peace, the abolition of landlordism; workers' control over production and the establishment of Soviet power – this cause has been secured.'

Later that day the second Congress of Soviets assembled at Smolny. The Bolsheviks and their allies were found to have a majority among the delegates who were present. The Mensheviks and Right Socialist Revolutionaries denounced the Bolshevik seizure of power then left the hall to the sound of Trotsky's invective: 'Go to the place where you belong from now on – the dustbin of history.'

Before the Congress adjourned early the next morning it heard of the fall of the Winter Palace. Lenin retired to a friend's apartment to sleep, before composing the first two pieces of legislation for the new government: the Decrees on Peace and Land.

Why was the uprising successful? The Menshevik, Isaac Steinberg, believed that:

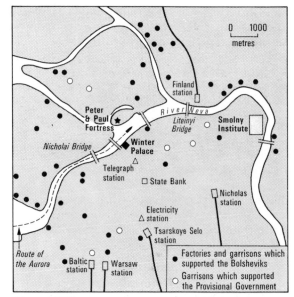

Petrograd, 1917

'October was accomplished . . . apparently by the actions of a definite party but it was at the same time prepared by all the unfolding events hitherto. . . . The army, exhausted by a desperate thirst for peace and anticipating all the horrors of a new winter campaign, was looking for a decisive change in policy. The peasantry, yearning for freed land and fearing to lose it in incomprehensible delays, was also waiting for this change. The proletariat, having seen lock outs, unemployment and the collapse of industry and dreaming of a new social order . . . awaited this change, and finally, vast innumerable circles of the population, "the men in the street", stifled by the atmosphere of political and military uncertainty, were also awaiting the easing of this atmosphere.'

The Bolsheviks had seized power. Could they hold

87

it? Already the deposed Prime Minister Kerensky was marching on the capital with troops in an attempt to restore his discredited regime.

Red Army street patrol during the October Revolution, 1917

Assignment

1 From which areas did the Bolsheviks gain their support?
2 For what reasons did Zinoviev and Kamenev oppose Lenin's decision to try to seize power?
3 What part did Trotsky play in the events leading to the Bolshevik uprising?
4 Outline the actions taken by Kerensky on 4–5 November.
5 Describe the events of 6–7 November including the taking of the Winter Palace.
6 Why was the Bolshevik Revolution successful?

Chapter Eleven

The Soviet government in power

Forming the New Government

On 8 November 1917 the second All-Russian Congress of Soviets met in full session and handed over power to the newly created Soviet Council of People's Commissars – Sovnarcom. The Chairman was Lenin and its fourteen Commissars included Trotsky, in charge of Foreign Affairs, Rykov, Internal Affairs and Stalin, in charge of Nationalities.

Lenin's first major task was to bring Russia's involvement in World War I to an end. He called upon all belligerent nations to start negotiations for a just and democratic peace:

> 'By a just and democratic peace . . . the
> government means an immediate peace without
> annexations . . . and without indemnities. . . .
> The government abolishes secret diplomacy . . .
> and will immediately proceed to the full
> publication of the secret treaties.'

At first, Lenin hoped that the German troops, sick of war and inspired by the Russian example, would refuse to fight. This did not happen and Russia was obliged to seek an armistice which was signed on 5 December, 1917. Peace negotiations then began at the Polish town of Brest-Litovsk.

Making Peace The German government was represented at the peace talks by their Foreign Minister, von Kuhlmann, while General Hoffman appeared on behalf of the German Army. Hoffman was anxious that the Germans take advantage of their military superiority and impose a severe peace on the Russians as speedily as possible. The Austrians were represented by Count Ottokar Czernin, who was as desperate for peace as the Russians themselves. He realized that, if the negotiations broke down, the collapse of the Austro-Hungarian Empire could not be long delayed. The Russian representative was Joffe, who conducted the negotiations until 27 December when Trotsky arrived in person to present the case for the Soviet government.

Trotsky at Brest-Litovsk

Trotsky's bargaining position was hopelessly weak as:

1 The Russian Army had melted away and their front line was undefended.
2 Russia's war-time allies refused to recognize the Soviet regime and were totally opposed to any Russian withdrawal from the War, as it released German troops to fight in the West and endangered the stocks of war materials which the Allies had sent to Russia.
3 The Ukraine had declared itself an independent Republic and insisted on its right to make a separate peace with the Central Powers, which they signed 9 February 1918.

Trotsky, like Lenin, believed that Bolshevik-style revolutions would soon break out in Germany and in central Europe and tried to spin out the negotiations. He proposed that Russia withdraw from the war but refuse to sign the peace settlement – 'no war, and no peace'. The Germans regarded this as unsatisfactory and launched an offensive against the Russian positions. Lenin now insisted that the German terms must be accepted if the Soviet regime was to survive, although he realized that many Russians were angry at the signing of the Treaty:

'Our impulse tells us to rebel, to refuse to sign this robber peace. Our reason will in our calmer moments tell us the plain naked truth – that Russia can offer no physical resistance because she is materially exhausted by a three years' war.... The Russian Revolution must sign the peace to obtain a breathing space to recuperate for the struggle.'

Terms of Treaty of Brest-Litovsk

1 Russia had to withdraw all troops from Poland, Latvia, Lithuania, Estonia and Finland.

Treaty of Brest-Litovsk

2 Russia had to make a separate peace with the Ukraine and withdraw all Soviet troops as a prelude to a German occupation of the region.
3 Russia had to pay 6,000 million gold marks in war damages.

Consequences of Brest-Litovsk Russia lost 62 million of her population, one-quarter of her territory, one-third of her agricultural land, more than half of her industry, and had to pay a vast sum in war damages at a time when the country was in chaos. The Treaty was a shattering blow to the Russian economy, especially the loss of the vital grain, sugar, coal and iron resources of the Ukraine; grain badly needed by starving Russian towns.

The Allies bitterly resented the Russian withdrawal from the war; German troops were freed for the Western Front at a critical stage of the war there, and supplies of food from the Ukraine helped to alleviate starvation, and therefore the threat of revolution, within Germany itself. The result was that the Allies sent troops to intervene in Russia itself, on the pretext of protecting Allied war supplies.

Many Russians opposed the Bolsheviks because of their acceptance of peace at any price. But Lenin had little choice but to accept the terms since Russia was in no state to defend herself. He had pledged peace, and most Russians wanted the slaughter to stop, no matter what the cost.

The settlement gave the new Soviet government a valuable breathing space; time to organize the administration, consolidate itself in power, and to begin to rebuild the army.

Assignment

1 What do you understand by the phrase 'a peace without annexation and indemnities'?
2 Why did the Allies refuse to recognize the new Soviet government?
3 Why was Trotsky in a weak bargaining position at Brest-Litovsk?
4 What justification did Lenin have for describing the Treaty of Brest-Litovsk as a robber peace?
5 Was it necessary for the Soviet government to accept Brest-Litovsk? Give reasons for your answer.

The Elimination of Political Opposition

The Constituent Assembly After military opposition to the Bolsheviks had been defeated in northern and central Russia the opponents of the new regime rested their hopes on the elections for the Constituent Assembly which the Provisional Government had fixed for 25 November. Lenin, who had no time for 'bourgeois democracy', wanted to postpone the elections but he was overruled by his colleagues who felt it politically unwise to cancel or delay the election so soon after they had come into power.

The results of the election were as follows:

Bolsheviks	175
Left S.R.s	40
Social Revolutionaries	370
Kadets	17
Mensheviks	16
Various National Parties	86
Others	3

Although the total vote was unfavourable to the Bolsheviks there was no unity among the opposition parties as the Bolshevik vote was strong in

Voting for the Constituent Assembly

those places which were strategically most important, in Petrograd, in Moscow, in the Baltic Fleet and at the fronts nearest the capital. The Constituent Assembly had its only meeting on 18 January 1918, and elected the moderate S.R. leader, Victor Chernov as its President. A.B. Ulam describes the scene:

'Soldiers and sailors, workers and peasants invaded the public galleries. People were shouting at the top of their voices, trying to argue above the din. . . . Inside the hall began to resemble a battlefield. Chairs and tables were overturned, pictures torn from the walls, in every row there were groups of soldiers trying to heckle the speakers, their rifles cocked threateningly towards the platform.'

The delegates eventually dispersed at 4 a.m. agreeing to reconvene at noon. But the next session was never held. On 19 January the Soviet Executive Committee published a decree dissolving the Constituent Assembly on the grounds that it threatened the power of the Soviets and served as a cover for 'bourgeois counter-revolution'. Red Guards were stationed round the Tauride Palace to prevent entry

and Russia's one-day experiment with Parliamentary democracy disappeared amid popular indifference and apathy.

The CHEKA and the Red Terror On 20 December 1917 there was founded the Extraordinary Commission – the CHEKA – whose function was:

'To cut off at the roots all counter-revolution and sabotage in Russia; to hand over to the revolutionary court all who are guilty of such attempts; to work out measures for dealing with such cases; and to enforce these measures without mercy . . .'

At its head was a Polish communist with long experience of Tsarist prisons and the methods of the *Okhrana*, Felix Dzerzhinsky. At first this new secret police had no power to execute, but by January 1918 Lenin had announced: 'we can achieve nothing unless we use terror'. By February *Pravda* announced that the CHEKA could 'see no other method of fighting counter-revolutionaries, spies, speculators, looters, hooligans, saboteurs and other parasites than their merciless destruction on the spot'.

The only session of the Constituent Assembly, Tauride Palace, Petrograd.

Dzerzinsky: head of the CHEKA, in charge of the Red Terror

Red Terror: the CHEKA parade a banner 'In the struggle with economic ruin there is no limitation on working time.'

The attempt on Lenin's life which led to an intensification of the Terror.

This wave of Red Terror was directed firstly against 'class enemies' but increasingly against all enemies of the Party, including members of other socialists groups. Press censorship had been reintroduced as early as November 1917, and non-socialist papers had been banned. In December, members of the Kadet Party were branded 'enemies of the people' and in the following month two of their leaders were lynched.

In the summer of 1918 the Royal Family were executed but it was the assassination of Uritsky, a leading Bolshevik, and the near fatal shooting of Lenin by the Socialist Revolutionary terrorist, Fanny Kaplan, which brought about an intensification of the Terror. The Commissar for Internal Affairs, Petrovsky, issued the following instruction:

'There must be an end of laxity and weakness. . . . Mass shooting must be applied upon the least attempts at resistance or the least movement in the midst of the White Guards.'

Accurate figures of those eliminated by the CHEKA are not available and estimates of those killed during the Red Terror vary from 50,000 to half a million. It must be remembered that the Bolsheviks did not hold a monopoly on terror. Hundreds of thousands of Soviet sympathizers were shot during this period by the White Armies and their supporters.

The Rallying of Support But the Bolshevik government could not have survived unless it had taken positive steps which gained the approval of the great mass of Russian people.

The first step was the Decree on Land which

recognized the fact of land seizures by the peasants and granted the formal right of ownership, to peasant families, of the land they worked and the crops they harvested.

Industry was not totally nationalized until the middle of 1918 but a decree of 14 November 1917 gave the State the right to confiscate any business which did not agree to workers control. In the meantime those industries which accepted workers committees continued operations under the supervision of their former owners and managers.

The government then embarked on a systematic attack on private property and private wealth. In December 1917 the right of the private ownership of large houses was abolished and the buildings turned over to the local Soviets, who moved in working class families. All banks were nationalized and the former private banks merged with the State Bank. In January 1918 all payments of dividends and dealings in shares were declared illegal, and in February the government announced its refusal to honour any of its debts, including those to foreign governments or investors. Wages, salaries and pensions were all reduced and Commissars were paid on a level with skilled workers. The rich were obliged to give huge sums in 'loans' to the government.

The reforms of the Bolshevik government were not confined to economic matters. In December 1918 the old marriage and divorce laws were swept away. Only civil marriages were recognized by the State. Divorce was made extremely easy and women were given legal equality with men. The Russian alphabet was simplified and the old Russian calendar, thirteen days behind the West, was discarded. The Churches were denied the right to own property and religious education in schools was forbidden.

In the courts, old judges were removed from office and replaced by new ones elected by the Soviets or by popular vote. Revolutionary tribunals, elected by Soviets, were set up to deal with cases of counter-revolution and sabotage.

Freedom was granted to all the subject peoples of the old Russian Empire. Each new republic was to have its own government and be permitted to use its native language in local schools.

In the Army, ranks were abolished and the control of the forces was handed over to soldiers' committees, but this situation was not to last long as the danger posed by Civil War required the creation of an efficient fighting force with which to defend the Revolution.

Suppression of religion: Red Guards plunder a church.

Sverdlov, Party organizer

At the seizure of power in November 1917 there were perhaps a quarter of a million Bolshevik Party members. By March 1921 there were over 700,000 Communists. This highly disciplined, unified group saw itself as the elite of the working class: 'The Communist Party is part of the working class: its most progressive, most class conscious and therefore most revolutionary part.'

All government power in Russia became con-

'Lenin cleans the Earth of evil spirits'. Can you identify them?

ТОВ. Ленин ОЧИЩАЕТ ЗЕМЛЮ ОТ НЕЧИСТИ.

The Communist Party The Soviet government could not have survived but for the existence of the Party; that 'tightly organized group of half a million communists, bound together by common hopes, common ideals, common hates'. It possessed a strong and gifted leadership. The untiring Lenin was undoubtedly the decisive figure but there was also Trotsky, organizer of the Red Army; Zinoviev, Party boss in Petrograd and head of the Third International; Kamenev, party head in Moscow; Dzerzhinsky, the head of the CHEKA; Sverdlov, until his early death, the Party organizer and others including Stalin, Rykov and Bukharin.

centrated in the hands of the Party. All political opposition including Mensheviks and Socialist Revolutionaries were suppressed, imprisoned, exiled or shot. The trade unions, the co-operatives, even the Soviets themselves lost all independent power and became mere agents of the Party. In Russia between 1917 and 1921 there developed the dictatorship of a single Party which tolerated no political opposition or criticism and constantly conducted propaganda on its own behalf among the masses.

Party members who were corrupt or abused power were rooted out and disciplined, and centralized control became even tighter until, in March 1921, Lenin banned all factions or groups inside the Party and destroyed all hopes for inner party democracy.

Assignment

1 a) What was the purpose of a Constituent Assembly?
   b) Why do you think the Bolsheviks dissolved the Constituent Assembly?
2 a) What were the aims of the CHEKA and against whom were its activities directed?
   b) Why do you think there were attempts on Lenin's life?
3 What steps did the Bolshevik government take to gain the support of the poorer sections of Russian Society?
4 Is it true to say that 'in Russia between 1917 and 1921 there developed the dictatorship of a single party which tolerated no political opposition'? Give reasons for your answer.

Bolshevik poster celebrating the first anniversary of the Revolution: 'A year of Proletarian Dictatorship'. At the top of the poster the slogan of the Revolution: 'Proletarians of all countries unite!'

Chapter Twelve

Civil War, 1918–21

The Defence of Petrograd

The new Soviet government faced immediate problems. The success of the revolution in Moscow and the rest of Russia was still uncertain, and opposition to the new government was developing in the Ukraine and the Cossack regions.

Kerensky The most pressing problem was posed by Kerensky, the deposed Prime Minister, who was marching on Petrograd with an army under General Krasnov. Krasnov's Cossacks were driven back by Red Guards on 12 November and Kerensky was obliged to go into hiding until he was eventually able to leave Russia.

Moscow fell to the Bolsheviks in mid-November 1917, with the loss of some five hundred Red Guards, and by December the main towns and railway centres of north and central Russia and Siberia were in Soviet hands. Outside this area, however, confusion reigned as numerous anti-Bolshevik governments of widely differing political views were established.

Whites and Reds Those groups which were opposed to the Bolsheviks, for whatever reasons, became known as the Whites. These included:
1 Mensheviks and S.R.s opposed to the dissolution of the Constituent Assembly.
2 Kadets and other groups who objected to Brest-Litovsk and wished to continue the war against Germany.

3 Land-owners whose estates had been seized or handed over to the peasants, under the terms of the Land Decree.
4 Factory owners and businessmen whose property had been nationalized under War Communism and, like other former wealthy groups, were now subject to compulsory and often menial labour.
5 Devout members of the Orthodox Church who viewed the Bolsheviks as militant atheists bent on destroying organized religion.
6 Former supporters of the Provisional Government and royalists who wished to restore the monarchy.
7 The Czech Legion who wished to leave Russia to continue the war against the Germans.

These elements in Russian society provided the support for the three major White Armies which emerged to fight the Bolsheviks: the Siberian Army of Admiral Kolchak with its headquarters at Omsk; the North-Western Army of General Yudenich based in Estonia; the Volunteer Army of General Denikin based in the Cossack regions of southern Russia.

Those who supported the Bolshevik government were known as the Reds. These included:

1 Factory workers in the towns and cities.
2 Former soldiers and sailors of the Tsarist army and navy.
3 Peasants conscripted into the new Red Army.

Civil War: the main campaigns

The Red Army

Soviet defeats in the Ukraine and the Don in the spring of 1918 demonstrated the need to create a new force to defend the Revolution. The 7,000 Red Guards of November 1917 were to become by 1920 a Red Army of over 5,000,000. This new force was the creation of Trotsky who became Commissar for War in March 1918.

Trotsky reintroduced conscription by first calling up industrial workers from Moscow and Petrograd, to give the Red Army a solid working class base and later, the less reliable peasants. By the end of 1918 the Red Army was 800,000 strong.

Trotsky as War Commissar The success of the Red Army became bound up with the career of Trotsky. He raced from one fighting front to another dictating orders, reviving the spirits of the

Soviet propaganda poster: 'Beware of Mensheviks and S.R.s – behind them come Tsarist generals, priests and landowners.' (left)
The Red Army: training of workmen (below left) public parade in Red Square Moscow (above), and its creator, War Commissar Trotsky, addressing Red Army soldiers (below)

troops, issuing military honours and leaving instructions for the execution of traitors and deserters. Trotsky's armoured train (the train of the Predrevoyensoviet) became a symbol of the Revolution at war and ultimately of the Red Army victory.

'Its sections included a secretariat, a printing press, a telegraph station, a radio station, an electric power station, a library, a garage and a bath.'

The Need for Officers   Trotsky then decided that elected soldiers' committees could not lead regiments into battle and admitted that although 'the Tsar's officers had been driven out of the old army quite ruthlessly; we had to enrol them as instructors for the Red Army . . .'

Over 48,000 ex-Tsarist officers served in the Red Army during the Civil War. Many Bolsheviks objected to these officers believing, often rightly, that they would desert or betray their own troops at the earliest opportunity. Trotsky took steps to ensure the loyalty of any officers tempted to desert to the Whites: 'I order the staffs of all armies . . . [take] necessary measures for the detention of the families of deserters and traitors.'

Political Commissars   Bolshevik Party Members were placed at every level of the military ladder as Political Commissars. They were reponsible for the moral and political education of the troops and the loyalty of the commander. Trotsky held both commissar and commander equally responsible for the discipline and fighting spirit of the troops.

But victory for the Bolsheviks seemed distant in 1918. The Germans occupied Poland, Latvia and Lithuania. The Ukraine had become an Austro-German colony and the Czech Legion had seized control of the Trans-Siberian Railway. Troops from Britain, France, Japan and the United States had landed in Russia and were giving aid to the enemies of the Soviet regime. Peasant armies had arisen which fought both Reds and Whites, and the Whites themselves were forming into three main anti-Bolshevik armies.

The Early Campaigns In mid-December 1917 the Soviet government turned its attention towards the Ukraine and the Cossack regions. Lenin dispatched Antonov-Ovseenko, the victor of the Winter Palace, south to Kharkov to begin operations. By early February 1918 Kiev and the other major Ukrainian towns had been taken by Red troops, under a former Tsarist officer named Muraviev. This early success was short-lived for, by March, they were obliged to evacuate the Ukraine in the face of an advance by German troops. Antonov had more success against the Cossacks, and by the end of February the Don region was in Bolshevik hands. There was a brief lull in the fighting until May 1918 when the Soviet regime faced its first major threat – the revolt of the Czech Legion.

The Revolt of the Czechoslovak Legion

In 1914 the provinces of Bohemia and Slovakia were part of the ·Austro-Hungarian Empire but many of their inhabitants, later called Czechoslovaks, wanted to set up their own national state.

On the outbreak of war many Czechs had joined a brigade attached to the Russian Army. In the summer of 1917 the Czech Nationalist leader, Masaryk, visited Russia to try to recruit volunteers from the ranks of Czech prisoners of war. He succeeded in creating a separate Czech Legion of around 40,000 men.

After November 1917 when it became clear that Lenin was determined to make a separate peace with Germany, Masaryk decided to transport the Legion to Vladivostok and from there by ship to France, in order to continue their fight against the Germans and Austrians. The disorderly state of the country and delays on the Trans-Siberian Railway, led to a rapid deterioration in relations between the Czechs and the Bolshevik authorities.

The Chelyabinsk Incident A minor incident in the station at Chelyabinsk, in western Siberia in May 1918, brought about the open revolt of the Czech Legion. A train carrying a Czech unit eastwards met a train carrying Hungarian prisoners of war westwards. A Hungarian threw a crowbar and killed a Czech. A scuffle followed and a Hungarian was killed. The local Soviet then arrested several Czechs whom it believed to be responsible for the death. The rest of the Czech unit then marched into Chelyabinsk, disarmed the local Red Guards, arrested the Soviet and took possession of the town.

On 25 May Trotsky instructed 'All Soviets on

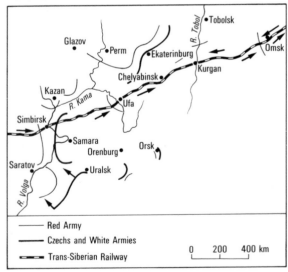

The confusion of fronts in the summer of 1918.

100

the railroad line ... to disarm the Czechoslovaks. Every Czech who is found armed on the railroad is to be shot on the spot.'

But the local Soviets lacked the power to carry out these instructions and by late June the Legion controlled the Trans-Siberian Railway from Penza to Vladivostok. The Allied governments now decided that the Czechs should remain in Russia, to provide a rallying point for all anti-Bolshevik forces and to pave the way for a more extensive foreign intervention. The Czechs advanced as far as the cities of Simbirsk and Kazan before they were halted by Red Army counter-attacks in September 1918.

The Czechs Withdraw With the end of the First World War, in November 1918, the Czechoslovaks no longer had any wish to remain in Russia and, although they remained in Siberia until 1920, they ceased to play an active part in the Civil War. Nevertheless they had struck the Soviet regime a severe blow at the time when its forces were at their weakest, and had made possible the setting up of anti-Bolshevik governments over large areas of Russia.

The Captivity and Execution of the Royal Family

Captivity After his abdication in March 1917 Nicholas Romanov and his family were sent to Tsarskoye Selo while the Provisional Government considered their future. The British government agreed to grant them sanctuary in March 1917, only to withdraw the offer in April in the face of a hostile British public. The July Days persuaded Kerensky of the need to remove the Royal Family from the threat of a revolutionary Petrograd and, in August, the Romanovs were sent to the remote Siberian town of Tobolsk.

After the Bolshevik revolution the situation of

Ex-Tsar Nicholas chopping wood at Tobolsk, winter 1917

the Royal Family became worse. They were obliged to dismiss most of their servants and their food supplies were reduced. In late April 1918 they were moved to Ekaterinburg in the Urals, where their hardships increased and they were subjected to increasingly hostile treatment by their Bolshevik guards.

On 12 July, the Ural Soviet decided that the presence of the Royal Family could no longer be tolerated in Ekaterinburg, as the town was under threat by Czech and White Russian forces. Jacob Yurovsky, a member of the Ural Soviet, was commissioned to carry out the killing of the former Imperial Family and their servants.

The Execution On the night of 16 July, Yurovsky, aided by CHEKA agents Ermakov and Varganov and Latvian soldiers, awakened the Romanovs and told them to dress. On the pretext of

The scene of the execution of the Royal Family.

disturbances in the town, they were escorted to the basement to await, in safety, the arrival of transport. Yurovsky said to the Tsar 'Your men have tried to save you but haven't succeeded, and we are forced to put you to death.'

Then the whole family were executed. The corpses were taken to an abandoned mine near the village of Koptyaki some 21 km. from Ekaterinburg where, with the help of great quantities of benzine and sulphuric acid, all evidence of the bodies was destroyed.

Results of the Execution The whole affair is shrouded in doubt, especially as the bodies have never been found. The Soviet government denied responsibility for the assassinations and arrested 28 men of whom 5 were executed for their part in the murders. Trotsky later claimed that Lenin and Sverdlov ordered the assassinations, early in July, to prevent the Royal Family from becoming symbols of the counter-revolution. Whatever the truth of the murders, the fact remained that the Royal Family were never seen again and their removal conveniently solved a difficult problem for the Soviet regime.

Assignment

1 What type of people supported the White Armies and for what reasons?
2 Why do you think Trotsky first conscripted industrial workers into the Red Army?
3 Why was it necessary to employ ex-Tsarist officers in the Red Army, and what steps were taken by Trotsky to ensure the loyalty of these officers?
4 What do you think was the significance of the Czechoslovak involvement in the Russian Civil War?
5 Why were the deaths of the Royal Family desirable from the point of view of the Soviet government?

Admiral Kolchak

In September 1918 Trotsky's new Red Armies gained important victories at Kazan and Samara and moved east of the Volga, but by November they were faced with more formidable opposition. A military dictatorship had been set up at Omsk in eastern Siberia under the former naval commander and Arctic explorer, Admiral Kolchak.

Kolchak was brave and patriotic and pursued a simple programme: 'I set as my main objective the creation of an efficient army, victory over Bolshevism and the establishment of law and order.' Unfortunately he was also nervous and highly strung, and lacked balanced judgement.

His former career as a naval officer did not fit him for the role of popular leader. Kolchak could only hope to defeat Bolshevism if he could gain popular support inside both Siberia and the Bolshevik territory, for he suffered serious geographi-

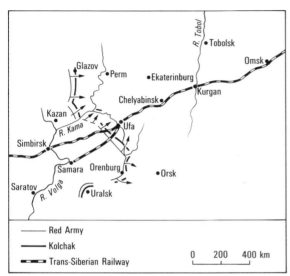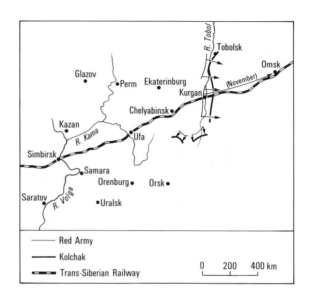

Kolchak's campaigns: May 1919 (left), August 1919 (right)

cal disadvantages. Under his rule were almost 12 million people scattered over a huge area of undeveloped territory; while the Soviet government had control of a compact and industrialized area containing over 60 millions. A naval expert, Kolchak knew nothing of land warfare and made his ultimate success unlikely by choosing incompetent generals.

Kolchak's Campaigns Kolchak's forces were divided into two. By December 1918 his Northern Siberian army had captured Perm and by the following March the Western Army had taken Ufa and was threatening Kazan and Samara.

Despite these early successes serious shortcomings became apparent in Kolchak's campaign. There was little co-operation between the two armies and there were quarrels over the allocation of supplies. In late April 1919 the advance of the Western Army was halted by strong Red forces which continued to drive the White Armies back

from the Volga. The Siberian Army had, by early June, reached Glazov. Thereafter, it was forced into a retreat which soon collapsed into a disorderly rout. The White Armies began to break up. There was widespread desertion and many of Kolchak's troops crossed over to the Bolsheviks.

The Red Army entered Omsk, Kolchak's capital, in November 1919 and the dictator was forced to flee eastwards. In January 1920 he surrendered himself to the Czechs at Irkutsk and was promptly imprisoned. The Czechs then handed him over to the Soviet authorities in Irkutsk who intended to put him on trial but, faced with the threat of new White Armies from the east, decided on his speedy execution. He was shot by firing squad on 7 February 1920.

Kolchak: Reasons for failure Kolchak's failure was not merely a result of military defeat. Dictatorial rule by military officers led to widespread brutality and instant justice, which turned many

Kolchak (centre) with the commanders of the Czech Legion, Omsk, 1919

ЗА ЕДИНЯЮ РОССИЮ

This Pro-White poster 'For a united Russia' shows Kolchak's Siberian army saving Russia from the Bolshevik dragon.

against Kolchak's government.

The harshness of the authorities, the compulsory recruitment of peasants into Kolchak's armies, the burden of taxation, all helped to bring about the formation of peasant bands (called partisans) which frequently disrupted the rear of Kolchak's forces by their seizure of the Trans-Siberian Railway. Devoted to the idea of restoring law and order, Kolchak was unable to check the brutal excesses of the soldiers who had brought him into power and, by antagonizing the population he was trying to win, he was fore-doomed to failure.

Denikin

The Volunteer Army The first White Army had been formed, in the Don regions, by Generals Kornilov, Denikin and Alekseev, the former Tsarist Chief-of-Staff. It attracted into its ranks many veteran officers and aristocrats, who were bitterly anti-Bolshevik, but who were welcomed in the Cossack regions where the inhabitants, with their large farms, were hostile to the land reforms and the food requisitioning associated with the Soviet regime. This Volunteer Army had, by the spring of 1919, driven the Red Army out of the Kuban and north Caucasus regions and had occupied key towns in the eastern Ukraine.

In July 1919 Denikin decided on a three-pronged attack on Moscow. White forces, under

Denikin's drive to Moscow, 1919

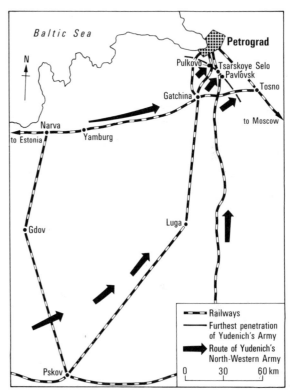

Yudenich: 20 October 1919.

Baron Wrangel, were to advance up the Volga; Sidorin, the Don Cossack commander, was to strike north-westwards and General Mai-Maevsky was to move north from Kharkov and west from Kiev. Denikin's armies advanced rapidly, and by 13 October had reached Orel, 400 kilometres from Moscow. The next day *Pravda* wrote: 'Now even the blind see that the decisive days of the Revolution have come.'

Yudenich and the North-Western Army

In October 1919 when the Soviet authorities were concentrating on the threat posed by Denikin in the south, a sudden and unexpected attack was launched on Petrograd by the Russian North-Western Army under General Yudenich. In many ways this was a foolish undertaking, as Yudenich was outnumbered by Red troops and Petrograd itself was full of Soviet sympathizers. He had little hope of gaining support from the local population or of receiving help from other White forces, and his lines of communication were open to attack by Red forces stationed to the south of Petrograd.

Yudenich's Advantages Certain factors however, did favour Yudenich. The 7th Red Army, although more numerous was spread out over a longer front. Its troops were of poor quality; their morale had been weakened by the chronic food shortages in the Petrograd area, while their Chief-of-Staff, Colonel Lunquist, was a White agent who encouraged desertions and informed Yudenich of Soviet troop positions and defensive weaknesses. Yudenich also received a few tanks and some naval support from the British.

The Attack on Petrograd By 16 October Yudenich had captured Gatchina, 50 kilometres south-west of Petrograd, and the Red forces were in retreat. His plan was to isolate Petrograd by cutting its rail links with the outside world. Two of the lines were successfully cut, but the failure of a unit commander to occupy Tosno station left the vital Petrograd-Moscow line under Bolshevik control. This was to prove a costly mistake.

The Defence of Petrograd Lenin at this time was prepared to let Petrograd fall to Yudenich, rather than allow troops to be diverted from defending Moscow against Denikin, but Trotsky believed the city could be saved without weakening the southern front, and arrived in person to organize the resistance. He improved morale, strengthened the 7th Army by rushing reinforcements from Moscow by rail, and laid plans for street fighting should the Whites enter the city. Barricades were put up in working class districts; partisan groups were organized and the Putilov workers hastily improvised a few tanks.

The Retreat of Yudenich By 20 October Yudenich had reached the Pulkovo Heights on the outskirts of Petrograd, but within two days the White forces were being pushed back beyond Pavlovsk and Tsarskoye Selo. The North-Western Army was obliged to retreat further as the 15th Red Army moved up from the south and threatened Yudenich's line of retreat. By mid-November he was forced to cross into Estonia where his army was disarmed, imprisoned and disbanded. Petrograd was saved, but a crucial struggle was about to take

'We won't surrender Petrograd'. Red propaganda poster.

place on the 1,130 kilometre front which stretched from Kiev to Tsaritsyn.

Denikin: Retreat and Defeat

On the southern front, Denikin found his armies faced with Red forces which were superior in numbers of men, machine-guns and artillery, and which had shorter lines of supply operating out of

Soviet controlled territory. On 20 October a crucial battle took place, near Orel, when the Volunteer Army was defeated and forced back towards Kursk. On 24 October the whole cavalry of Mamontov was defeated, at Voronezh, by the Red cavalry corps under Budenny. These two battles marked the turning point of the southern campaign and from then onwards the initiative lay with the Red forces.

The retreat of the White Armies became a rout. Denikin's lines of supply were being constantly cut by peasant partisan bands, notably those of the

Denikin

Ukrainian anarchist, Makhno, while the lack of discipline within his forces made it impossible to hold them together in the face of continual defeats.

By mid-December the White Armies, now a disorderly rabble, had withdrawn either to the Crimea or to the Don. In early January 1920 Denikin made a stand at Rostov, but was obliged to withdraw south after a successful flanking movement by Budenny's Red Cavalry. A short-lived victory for the Whites at Bataisk held up the Bolshevik advance, but soon Denikin was again retreating; this time towards Novorossiysk on the Black Sea. Here, amid wild scenes of panic and disorder as thousands of civilian refugees tried to fight their way on board the ships, Denikin evacuated the remnants of the Volunteer Army to the Crimea. There he resigned his command in favour of Baron Wrangel and in April 1920 left Russia, to end his days in exile.

The Failure of White Government Denikin's failure was not merely a result of the overwhelming superiority of the Red Armies, but was also caused by his inability to win the support of the Russian masses. He was not a popular leader. He could not talk to the masses in language they understood nor could he offer them more appealing policies than the Bolsheviks he was fighting. Although no Monarchist he was no liberal, and most of his advisers were more reactionary than Denikin himself. As soon as White troops occupied new territory and a government was set up, the old officials, the old landlords and the old policemen returned. Such policies did not win over the peasants, many of whom had no love for the Bolsheviks; particularly their food detachments.

The discipline of the White Armies was often lax, and the behaviour of many soldiers and officers disreputable. Looting and corruption were widespread within the White ranks as even commanders like Wrangel were prepared to admit:

'The war has become a means of growing rich. . . . Many officers . . . are engaged in selling and trading loot. The army is completely demoralized and is rapidly turning into a bunch of tradesmen and profiteers.'

Another factor which hindered Denikin was his Russian nationalism. His slogan – 'Russia shall be great, united and undivided', might appeal to ex-Tsarist officers, former Imperial officials, landlords and businessmen, but it had little appeal to Ukrainians, Poles, Cossacks and Caucasian tribesmen, who preferred independence to the restoration of rule by Russians, of whatever political stamp.

Peasant Insurgents

Denikin's defeat was not simply a result of superior Red tactics and the demoralization of the White Armies. Part of the reason lay with the activities of the peasant armies operating in his rear.

In various parts of Russia, throughout the Civil War, peasant armies arose to fight against both Reds and Whites, when either threatened their particular region. The main factor in the hostility of the peasants was their determination to keep the land which they had seized throughout 1917. They therefore were quick to rebel when White Armies brought back the old landlords, but were equally opposed to the Bolsheviks, who wished to move them into state farms and communes, or who sent out detachments to make food requisitions. They hated also the forced conscriptions into both Red and White Armies. As one peasant General put it:

'Instead of land and liberty they violently impose on you the commune, the CHEKA and Moscow commissars . . . those who promise you a bright future exploit you, fight with you, take away your grain with arms in their hands, requisition your cattle . . .'

Nowhere was this peasant hostility so well developed as in the Ukraine. There the peasants were generally better off than in the rest of Russia and their opposition was combined with factors of race and nationality. They associated Bolshevism with Greater Russians and Jews, and despised Denikin for his unwillingness to concede the Ukraine's right to political independence. Many joined the armies of the Ukrainian nationalist leader Simon Petlura, and participated in the widespread slaughter of Jews during 1919, as well as fighting against Bolsheviks and the Volunteer Army.

Nestor Makhno This wave of peasant disorder was to bring into prominence a man who, for long periods of time, dominated the steppes of the southern Ukraine from Ekaterinoslav to the Sea of Azov: 'Nestor Makhno, boozing, swashbuckling, disorderly and idealistic, proved himself to be a born strategist of unsurpassed ability. The number of soldiers under his command ran at times into several tens of thousands.'

Makhno differed from the other Ukrainian peasant leaders in a number of ways. He was not a Ukrainian nationalist, nor a murderer of Jews. He was a theoretical anarchist who fought under the Black Flag and was opposed to any form of government.

It was during the autumn of 1919 that Makhno played his most significant role in the Civil War. During September and October he inflicted several defeats on Denikin's forces and, by seizing important railway junctions, cut off the Whites from their supply bases.

Makhno's victories were short-lived. He had to leave his headquarters, at Ekaterinoslav, as Deni-

Nestor Makhno

was obliged to cross into Romania and into exile.

Most peasant insurgent movements had only the most vague and confused political programmes. Usually they were spontaneous outbursts of destructive hatred, by a tormented population which felt that conditions were intolerable, but had no constructive ideas as to what form of government to set up instead.

Assignment

1 What reasons can you find to explain why the Siberian peasants rose in revolt against Kolchak's government?
2 Explain why Yudenich almost succeeded in capturing Petrograd.
3 What reasons can you suggest to explain the collapse of Denikin's armies in the autumn of 1919?
4 For what reasons did the peasant armies fight against
   a) the Whites
   b) the Red Army?
5 Why was the Ukraine a particular source of peasant disorders?

kin retreated and his army melted away. Makhno then turned against the Bolshevik food collectors and CHEKA agents, who arrived in the wake of the Red Armies, and throughout 1920 he moved about the Ukraine raiding Soviet administration centres. In the autumn of 1920 Makhno co-operated with the Red forces against Wrangel, but after Wrangel's defeat the Soviet armies were free to concentrate their efforts against the peasant insurgents. By August 1921 his forces were scattered and Makhno

Chapter Thirteen

Foreign intervention

During 1918–20 the Soviet government was faced with two additional threats to its authority: the intervention of Russia's former wartime allies, Britain, France, U.S.A. and Japan; and the invasion of Russia by the armies of the new Polish State under Marshal Pilsudski.

Allied Intervention

Russia had withdrawn from the First World War, under the terms of the Treaty of Brest-Litovsk, in March 1918. The Allied governments, unhappy with this decision, decided to send detachments of their own troops into Russia in order:

1 To prevent military stores, sent by the Allies to Russia, from falling into German hands, and to deny the Germans access to raw materials vital to the war effort.
2 To support any Russians willing to continue the war, in order to keep a German Army on the Eastern Front and thus prevent the Germans from transferring their troops to the West.
3 To intimidate the Bolsheviks, who had seized foreign-owned property and had refused to pay Russia's pre-war debts.
4 To contain the spread of Bolshevism into central and western Europe.

Other reasons, given at various times, included the need to prevent a Turkish-German advance towards India, to prevent the freeing of German prisoners held in Siberia and to deny the Germans the use of Russia's northern ports as U-boat bases.

The Extent of Foreign Aid to the Whites   Lenin naturally condemned Allied intervention:

'Anglo-French bandits are already shooting Russian workers on the Murmansk railway which they have seized. . . . They are cutting off the Russian people from their bread to force them to put their necks once more into the noose of the Paris and London stock exchanges.'

In reality very few Allied troops were actively involved against the Bolsheviks, but the amount of material given to the White Armies was substantial. The British, in particular, sent considerable quantities of arms and equipment. Kolchak received over 100,000 tons of military material and, according to Minister of War, Churchill, Denikin received 'A quarter of a million rifles, two hundred guns, thirty tanks and large masses of munitions and equipment . . . sent through the Dardanelles and the Black Sea to the port of Novorossiysk' and 'several hundred British officers and non-commissioned officers, as advisers, instructors, storekeepers and even a few aviators furthered the organization of his armies.' Yudenich too received British assistance, in the form of tanks and naval support, during his attack on Petrograd. Much of the equipment however, was never used against the Bolsheviks. Such was the corruption of many White officers that great quantities of British aid found its way onto the black market.

The British did not pursue a consistent policy with regard to intervention in Russia. Churchill

Allied intervention: Relief forces arrive at Archangel, 1919 (top)
Japanese forces encounter partisans, 1920 (above)
British forces leave Vladivostok for Omsk, 1918 (right)

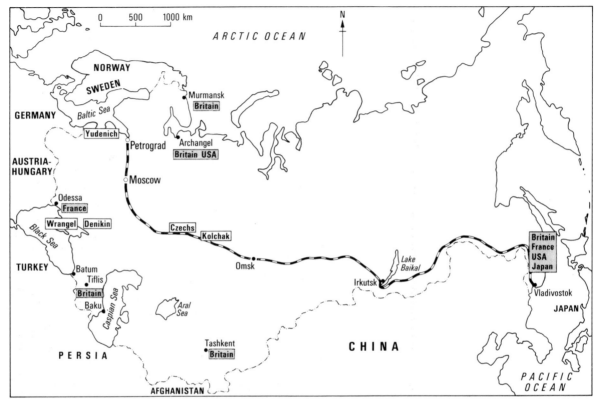

Areas of Allied intervention during the Russian Civil War

was anxious to crush Bolshevism by force. Anti-Russian feeling ran high in September 1918 when the British diplomat R. Bruce Lockhart was arrested by the CHEKA for his part in an alleged anti-Soviet plot, and Captain Cromie the naval attaché, was killed when CHEKA agents broke into the British Embassy. The Prime Minister, Lloyd George, was more concerned to defeat Germany than to interfere in the internal affairs of Russia. In February 1919 he informed Churchill:

'If Russia is really anti-Bolshevik then a supply of equipment would enable it to redeem itself. If

Russia is pro-Bolshevik, not merely is it none of our business to interfere with its internal forces, it would be positively mischievous. . . . An expensive war of aggression against Russia is a way of strengthening Bolshevism in Russia and creating it at home.'

The End of Allied Intervention   In the autumn of 1919 Archangel and Murmansk were evacuated. After the collapse of Kolchak's government in the winter of 1919–20 interventionist forces, with the exception of the Japanese, left Siberia. The British had left Baku and Tiflis in the summer of 1919 and in July 1919 they evacuated the south Caucasus. The French, who had intervened in the Ukraine and the Crimea, left with the defeat of Wrangel.

The Significance of Allied Intervention Allied intervention in the north was of little significance. Murmansk and Archangel were too remote from the main theatres of the Civil War, and the forces stationed there too small to have any impact. But it is true that the aid given to Kolchak and Denikin prolonged the existence of their armies, and that, had there been no Allied intervention, the Russian Civil War would have ended more quickly, with a decisive victory for the Soviet government. Intervention bought time for the peacemakers at Versailles to reconstruct central and eastern Europe during 1919 and 1920, and to prevent a victorious Red Army bringing revolution into the ruins of the Austro-Hungarian Empire at the point of a gun.

Churchill claimed that:

'A breathing-space of inestimable importance was afforded to the whole line of newly liberated countries which stood along the western borders of Russia. . . . Finland, Estonia, Latvia, Lithuania and, above all, Poland were able, during 1919, to establish the structure of civilized states and to organize the strength of patriotic armies.'

The Russo-Polish War of 1920

After the defeat of the White Armies and the withdrawal of the Allied interventionists the Soviet government's next problem was war with Poland.

Background At the start of the First World War, Poland did not exist as an independent nation; all her territories had been taken over by Russia, Austria and Prussia at the end of the eighteenth

Marshal Pilsudski

century. During the War, therefore, Poles had been conscripted into the armies of Russia, Austria, and Germany, and forced to fight against each other. The Polish nationalist leader, Jozek Pilsudski, was imprisoned by the Germans, but was released at the end of the War. He became head of the Independent Polish State which was set up under the terms of the Treaty of Versailles, June 1919.

Events of the Russo-Polish War Pilsudski wished to weaken Russia, by detaching the non-Russian territories of the old Tsarist Empire, and to create an independent Ukraine dependent on Poland. On 25 April Poles attacked the weak Soviet forces in the western Ukraine and the Reds, outnumbered and hindered by internal mutinies and the activities of peasant insurgents in their rear, offered little resistance, thus enabling the Polish forces to occupy Kiev on 6 May.

The Soviet forces were reorganized and reinforced, and counter-attacked on two fronts. On 14 May Red Armies, under Tukhachevsky, launched an attack through White Russia and forced back the Poles in the north. In the south, Soviet forces, spearheaded by Budenny's Red Cavalry, drove the Poles from Kiev on 12 June, and both wings embarked on a steady advance towards Poland.

On 12 July the British Foreign Secretary, Lord Curzon, warned the Soviet government that France and Britain would intervene if the Red Armies entered Polish territory. He proposed a ceasefire and suggested that the line of the River Bug should be accepted as the Russo-Polish frontier (the Curzon Line).

Marshal Budenny

Russo-Polish War 1920–1

The Red Armies continued their advance into Poland. Pilsudski and his French military adviser, General Weygand, decided to fight the Russians in front of Warsaw. A series of mistakes by the Soviet commanders, and a breakdown in communications between their armies, resulted in a gap opening up between the Red Armies, into which the Poles sent their troops. The Soviet advance was halted. Then on 16 August Pilsudski counter-attacked and drove first Tukhachevsky, then the other Red Armies back from Warsaw. This was the 'Miracle of the Vistula'. By the end of August Polish forces were again in western Russia and peace negotiations were begun at Riga.

114

The Treaty of Riga 1920–21 The Soviet government was anxious for a speedy settlement as it was anxious to turn the Red Armies against Wrangel, who had moved from the Crimea into the Ukraine taking advantage of the Soviet's pre-occupation with the Polish campaign.

By comparison with the territory held by the Poles in January 1920 the new frontier gave the Russians some 60,000 sq. km. and 4½ million people, but the new Soviet-Polish frontier was well to the east of the Curzon Line and stretched from Latvia to Romania. This gave to Poland territory populated by Ukrainians and White Russians, and effectively shut Russia off from direct contact with Lithuania and, through Lithuania, with Germany.

Wrangel: The Whites' Last Stand

In June 1920 Baron Peter Wrangel, taking advantage of the Soviet pre-occupation with the war against Poland, broke out of the Crimea and drove back the Red forces. As his army was too small to hold on to large territorial gains, he decided to move to the Cossack Kuban where there were rich reserves of grain and cattle. Despite early successes Wrangel was driven back to the Crimea by early September, by superior numbers of Soviet troops.

The Final Stages In October, Wrangel, after successful forays in the eastern Ukraine, decided to cross the River Dnieper to link up with the Polish forces which were again on the Ukrainian frontier. The attempt failed and the Whites were driven back with heavy losses. Wrangel's defeat was inevitable when the Poles agreed to a cease-fire thus permitting overwhelming numbers of Red Army soldiers to be mobilized against him. Outnumbered four to one, the White Army was driven back into the Crimea behind the fortifications on the Isthmus of Perekop. The struggle continued until the Red Army broke through on 11 November and scattered the White forces. Wrangel moved the remnants of his army to the Crimean ports and evacuated them, with some 150,000 civilians, to the safety of Constantinople. His defeat signified the end of White Russia.

Why the Bolsheviks Emerged Victorious

The end of the Polish war and the subsequent defeat of Wrangel marked the conclusion of the Civil War period. The holding of power by the Bolsheviks in those four years was a much greater achievement than their seizure of it in November 1917. It was also to be, in many ways, more formative of the subsequent character of Russian Communism.

How then was the Soviet government able to survive those terrible years and eventually emerge victorious?

Baron Wrangel

Генералъ-Лейтенантъ
ПЕТРЪ НИКОЛАЕВИЧЪ Баронъ ВРАНГЕЛЬ.

Российская Социалистическая Федеративная Советская Республика.
Пролетарии всех стран, соединяйтесь!

КРАСНЫЙ ПОДАРОК
БЕЛОМУ ПАНУ

ДВИНЬ-КА
ЭТИМ ЧЕМОДАН-
ЧИКОМ ПАНА В ЛОБ

This poster is entitled 'a Red present for the White overlord'.

The Bolsheviks, led by Lenin, Trotsky and Stalin, operated as a strongly disciplined, unified force (aided by the CHEKA and the Red Terror) able to mobilize the idealism of the young and of many of the industrial workers, while their opponents lacked a national leader and were hopelessly divided amongst themselves.

The Bolsheviks controlled the vital central region which included Moscow and Petrograd. They were able to operate on internal supply lines, using the rail network to strengthen whichever front seemed most threatened at any given time. In contrast, the White Armies were separated by vast distances and were unable to co-ordinate their attacks on the Soviet armies or to reinforce one another. Their troops frequently lacked discipline and had poor morale, while their links with the former land-owning class ensured the hostility of the peasant masses.

The Bolsheviks inherited the bulk of the war material which had been produced for use in the World War and this more than offset the munitions sent to the Whites by the Allies. The Allied interventionist forces were not prepared to directly fight the Bolsheviks and soon became disillusioned with their White Russian clients.

The Bolsheviks were able to win over many of the poorer peasants with promises of land, livestock and machinery, and to turn to advantage the intense class hatred which existed in the countryside. The peasant armies, although opposed to both Whites and Reds, were usually short-lived and unable to offer any real substitute for the Soviet government against which they were rebelling.

Assignment

1 Why did the Allies send troops to Russia?
2 What were the main results of Allied intervention?
3 Why did the Poles attack Russia?
4 Why were the Soviet Armies unable to conquer Poland?
5 Explain why Wrangel was doomed to defeat after October 1920.
6 Look back over the chapter and list all the reasons that you can find to explain the defeat of the White Armies.

Chapter Fourteen

War Communism

War Communism was a system developed between 1918 and 1921, partly as a response to the demands of the Civil War and partly as an attempt to leap into socialism, whereby the whole economic life of the country came to be directed by the State. By a series of decrees:

1 The State took over all the means of production including factories, mines, workshops and railways and reduced all types of private ownership by confiscating items of personal wealth.

2 The State set up a Food Commissariat which became the sole legal provider of food and manufactured goods. Food was requisitioned from the peasants and distributed among the population of the towns by a graded system of rationing, under which industrial workers received three times the amount allocated to professional men such as lawyers. Private trading was made illegal.

3 The State made work compulsory and all workers were made subject to government direction.

4 The State took over the banks, and attempted to abolish money by introducing a system of payment in goods and services.

War Communism in Action

In all areas of economic life (industry, agriculture and transport) production levels fell. The quality of goods produced deteriorated, while the productivity of labour declined drastically. Trade between countryside and towns virtually ceased and agriculture reverted to subsistence level. This overall economic collapse brought the Russian people to a level of misery and hardship unknown in western Europe during the harshest years of World War I.

Food The spread of the Civil War during 1918 made the collection of grain from the peasants, to feed the towns and the army, essential. But, as the Army absorbed the products of industry, there was little left to give the peasants in return. The peasants therefore preferred to sell their grain, not to the State but on the open (or black) market. Lenin outlined the problem in November 1919:

'The middle peasant produces more food than he needs and thus having surplus of grain becomes an exploiter of the hungry worker.... By no means all the peasants understand that free trade in grain is a state crime. "I produce the grain, it is my handiwork. I have the right to trade it." – that is how the peasant reasons.... And we say that this is a state crime.'

It became necessary to organize food detachments, made up of city workers, to go into the countryside to buy grain at fixed prices, or requisition it, from the peasants. Every food detachment was to be made up 'of not less than 75 men and two machine-guns'. Their function, according to Commissar for Agriculture, Tsyurupa, was twofold:

War Communism: a bread queue

'We do not regard these detachments merely as a military force; we see in these detachments . . . agitators who will conduct propaganda in the country . . .'

Half the grain obtained was given to the organization which sent out the detachment, the rest was handed over to the Food Commissariat for general distribution.

The peasants often reacted fiercely to the food detachments, and their expeditions were one of the main reasons for peasant hostility towards the Soviet government.

Not enough food reached the cities. Under the system of rationing even the favoured workers were only receiving about 10 per cent of the calorie intake of the British during the difficult wartime years of 1917–18, while the former wealthy or middle classes received practically nothing, and were likely to die of malnutrition or starvation unless they were able to trade some of their former possessions for food on the black market.

The Black Market Private trade had been made illegal, but more people engaged in it than ever before, despite confiscations and arrests. Much industrial material was stolen and sold, and workers turned to making penknives, cigarette lighters and items for household use, when they were supposed to be producing tools and machinery. Many Russians became 'speculators' as they could see no other way to effectively feed themselves or their families. Victor Serge, the revolutionary, later wrote in his memoirs:

'If you wished to procure a little flour, butter or meat from the peasants who brought these things illicitly into town, you had to have cloth or articles of some kind to exchange. Fortunately the town residences of the late bourgeoisie contained quite a lot in the way of carpets, tapestries, linen and plate. From the leather upholstery of sofas one could make passable shoes; from the tapestries, clothing.'

Fuel With a shortage of fuel for industry and transport little was left for homes or offices. In the cities wooden houses, sheds, fences and wooden pavings were pulled down and used for fuel. The Russian winter became a torture in revolutionary

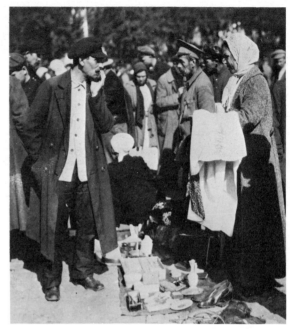

War Communism: fuel rationing (left), and the one-time rich sell their possessions to buy food. (right)

Petrograd. Thousands died of cold, or hunger or in the wave of typhus which swept the cities. Over most of the country normal life had become impossible.

Transport During the period of War Communism the transport system virtually ground to a halt. Trains, abandoned because of the Civil War or the lack of fuel, littered the tracks. The amount of rolling stock and the numbers of locomotives fit for service steadily declined:

Locomotives in service

1913	16,866	1919	4,577
1917	17,012	1920	3,969
1918	14,519	1921	7,683

Even when trains were available journeys were frequently uncertain:

'Trains nowadays often go unlighted, without regarding any of the regulations with regard to signals. . . . Moreover, the railcrews being not all interested in the exploitation of the railways, sometimes refuse to man the trains.'

Assignment

1 What do you understand by the phrase 'War Communism'?

2 Explain a) how food was obtained
b) how food was distributed under War Communism?

119

Chaos at Petrograd railway station, 1919

3 Describe how the peasants reacted to the food detachments.
4 Why did so many people make use of the black market?
5 What were the consequences of the fuel shortage?

Industry and Workers

Large-scale industry suffered the worst decline. Production was almost completely paralysed by the shortage of food, fuel, of metal and of skilled workers, while the output of small-scale industry declined proportionately less.

A major reason for this decline in industrial production was the wholesale flight from the starving towns to the countryside, where there was more chance of getting food. Between 1916 and 1920 the cities of north and central Russia lost over a third of their population, while the number of workers in industry declined by at least a half, as many returned to their native villages. However, despite the hardships, the low wages, the introduction of military discipline and the creation of labour armies, the workers remained remarkably loyal to the Soviet government. Certainly, opposition to the government and strikes led to visits by the CHEKA but there was no serious outburst of working class discontent until the winter of 1920–21.

Large-Scale Industrial Production (in million tons)

	1913	1921
Coal	29.0	8.9
Oil	9.2	3.8
Pig Iron	4.2	0.1
Steel	4.3	0.2
Rail Freight	132.4	39.4
Electricity (million kWh)	2039	420

Wages and the Productivity of Labour

	Wage per month in roubles	Productivity of labour
1913	22.00	100.0
1918	10.49	44.0
1919	8.47	21.6
1920	8.30	26.0

Reasons for the Failure of War Communism

There were three main reasons for the huge decline in production during 1917–21: the Civil War; the blockade of the country by the outside world; and the administration of the economy.

The Civil War Although the most important industrial regions of north and central Russia remained under Bolshevik control throughout the whole Civil War period, they were often cut off from the basic sources of raw materials and fuel for long periods of time. For example, the Moscow cotton industry was cut off from the cotton growing areas of Turkestan. The engineering works of Petrograd were cut off from the coal of the Donets Basin and iron of the Urals, while all sectors of industry were starved of Baku oil until the spring of 1920. As well as breaking up Russia's natural economic links the Civil War demanded a huge share of its scarce resources for the needs of the Red Army.

Foreign Blockade During the period 1917–21 Russia's foreign trade virtually ceased to exist. The country was blockaded by the Allies from the summer of 1918 until November 1920, thus depriving the country of foreign equipment, machinery and raw materials, and denying it access to alternative sources of supply of products cut off by the Civil War.

The Administration of War Communism The attempt by the State to nationalize everything, to

Famine on the Volga, 1921: feeding the children

Hungry peasants with their belongings on wagons, wander about Moscow in search of food.

A contemporary writer describes their condition:

'Their only shelter consists of strips of rags stretched from poles to the sides of the carts in which they have transported themselves and their belongings into the town. Usually there is no protection from the sky whatever. In these uncouth tents the whole family is herded together – old men with emaciated bodies, . . . women hardly able to step from one side of the shelter to the other, and children, innumerable children, sitting listlessly on the ground, too exhausted to move, to talk, to play . . . All through the summer they have watched the soil harden to stone under the rays of the terrible sun and the few scattered shoots which had pushed their heads through it blacken and perish. They had been living on the tiny remnants of the last year's harvest (which also was a failure) eked out with . . . acorns, bark, lime-tree leaves, pigweed, clay, insects beaten up into a paste, even animals' droppings – anything that will hold a modicum of flour together . . . And all the time they grow thinner and thinner; and some of them die and the rest get ready to follow them. On their faces is absolute despair.'

provision the population only through State agencies, led to the growth of a huge inefficient bureaucracy. The system was made worse by the dismissal of many former civil servants and their replacement by often uneducated and untrained Bolshevik supporters. Civil servants received little under the rationing system, and the virtual abolition of money destroyed the incentive to work and made it almost impossible to gauge the efficiency of the state-owned concerns. The Bolsheviks blamed failures on sabotage by White Agents, but often it was simply a result of muddle, incompetence and red tape.

The Results of War Communism By 1920 the country was cold, hungry, exhausted and bitter. Millions had died due to war, starvation and disease. Epidemics of typhus and cholera had ravaged the population and in 1920–21, after a severe drought, famine struck the Volga region, creating further misery as refugees moved from the stricken areas as best they could.

Assignment

1 What reasons can you suggest for the decline in the output of industry during the period of War Communism?

2 Which sectors of industry suffered the greatest decline 1913–1921?

3 Briefly outline the part played by each of the following in bringing about the decline in production
   a) The Civil War
   b) The Foreign Blockade
   c) The State Administration

Chapter Fifteen

The New Economic Policy

By the end of 1920 serious opposition to the policies associated with War Communism began to appear in many parts of the country.

Peasant Revolts

There had been peasant risings in western Siberia and, in Tambov province, a formidable army of peasants and bandits, under a self styled S.R. called Antonov, had arisen to resist the continuing food requisitions. Agricultural output was 30 per cent less than in 1913. The peasants had reduced the area under cultivation as a protest against the State which took their surplus produce and had forbidden them to engage in private trading. The peasants had also greatly reduced their stocks of livestock, while the production of non-food products such as cotton, flax, sugar beet and tobacco had almost ceased. This aggravated the food shortages in the towns and in January 1921, resulted in even more severe rationing of bread and fuel.

Workers' Discontent

As factories closed, for lack of fuel and shortages of labour, the discontent of many workers for the regime made itself felt. Within the Party itself a group called the Workers Opposition demanded a restoration of the rights of trade unions. At the same time many Russians felt that the Party had become full of bureaucrats and careerists and had lost touch with ordinary people.

In late February 1921 there was a short-lived wave of strikes in Petrograd which led to the city being placed under martial law, but the demands voiced by the workers were soon to be heard again.

The Kronstadt Rebellion

The single most important factor in persuading Lenin to abandon War Communism was the revolt of the sailors of the Baltic Fleet at the Kronstadt naval base. These sailors had played vital roles in both the November Revolution and the Civil War, and had been called the 'pride and glory of the Revolution'. In March 1921 however, they rose in rebellion against the repression and increasing dictatorship of the Soviet government, which they said had 'perverted the original ideals of the Revolution and had taken away its fruits from the workers and peasants in whose name it had been made'.

They demanded new elections for the Soviets, freedom of speech for other left-wing parties, freedom for trade unions, the release of left-wing political prisoners, the end of food requisitions and barrier searches, the right of peasants to hold land, and freedom of production for craftsmen.

The Defeat of Kronstadt On 5 March Trotsky announced the government's intention

'to bring Kronstadt and the mutinous ships into the possession of the Soviet Republic. All those

Attack on Kronstadt. Soviet forces cross the frozen waters of the Gulf of Finland.

who have lifted up hands against the socialist fatherland, lay down arms immediately . . . Only those who surrender unconditionally can count on the mercy of the Soviet Republic. At the same time orders are being given to make all preparations for the smashing of the mutiny and the mutineers by force of arms.'

Kronstadt refused to submit and hostilities began on 7 March and continued until the 17 March when the fortress fell to the Soviet forces. Hundreds of prisoners were taken and later shot by the CHEKA, but although the rebellion was crushed the warning of Kronstadt did not go unheeded. The demands for greater economic freedom for the peasants and the easing of the oppressive burdens felt by all citizens found a response in Lenin's speech to the Tenth Party Congress.

N.E.P.

In March 1921 Lenin announced the ending of War Communism and the inauguration of a New Econ-omic Policy. The basis of N.E.P. was:

1 The ending of requisitions from the peasants and the substitution of a fixed tax in kind (grain) – which by 1924 had become a money tax. Once this tax was paid the peasant was free to do what he liked with what remained. He could use it himself, sell it to the State or sell it on the open market which was now made legal.
2 Private enterprise was allowed in trade and small-scale industry.
3 Compulsory labour ceased; the labour armies were disbanded and bonuses were introduced for extra work.
4 The Currency was put back on a sound footing and a regular system of taxation was introduced.

Large-scale industry (coal, iron, steel, oil, electricity, railways) was to remain in the hands of the State.

Opposition to N.E.P. There were those in the Party who opposed N.E.P. because it was contrary to the principles of Marxist socialism. Lenin claimed that it was a temporary retreat (a step back to capitalism in order to re-group their resources for the final advance towards socialism) to give the Russian economy time to recover. Lenin outlined his thinking to the Party in April 1921:

'The civil war of 1918 greatly increased the devastation of the country, retarded the restoration of its productive forces, and bled the proletariat more than any other class. To this was added the failure of the harvest of 1920, the fodder shortage, the dying off of cattle, which still further retarded the restoration of transport and industry, because among other things, it interfered with employment of peasants' horses for carting wood, our main fuel . . .

We were forced to resort to "War Communism" by war and ruin . . . it was a temporary measure. We are still in such a state of ruin . . . that we cannot give the peasant manufactured goods for ALL we require. Knowing this we are introducing the tax in kind i.e. we shall take the minimum of grain we require (for the army and the workers) in the form of a tax and will obtain the rest in exchange for manufactured goods. . . . Our poverty and ruin are so great we cannot hope to restore large-scale factory state socialist production at one stroke. . . .

Hence, it is necessary, to a certain extent, to help to restore SMALL industry . . . the effect will be the revival of the petty bourgeois specialists, including merchants, small capitalist co-operation and capitalists.'

The Results of N.E.P. Lenin's main aim was to persuade the peasants to produce more food for the towns, and in this N.E.P. was largely successful. Agricultural production increased and by 1925 had reached pre-war levels. The richer peasants (*kulaks*) flourished and were allowed, after 1925, to employ hired labour.

Agricultural Land Area and Production

	Sown area (million hectares)	Grain harvest (million tons)
1913	105.0	80.0
1922	77.7	50.3
1925	104.3	72.5

The peasants also increased their holdings of livestock during N.E.P.

Livestock Holdings (in millions)

	Horses	Cattle	Pigs
1916	35.5	58.9	20.3
1922	24.1	45.8	12.0
1925	27.1	62.1	21.8

But as agricultural production increased it became clear that local markets were inadequate to cope with the growth of trade. A class of so-called N.E.P. men came into existence, who acted as middle men between countryside and towns, and by 1923 controlled 75 per cent of Russia's retail trade. After 1924 high prices were paid for agricultural products as the government offered the incentive of high profits to increase food production. This in turn led to the development of small-scale private industry to provide consumer goods on which the peasants might spend their profits; while currency reserves were used to buy tractors from abroad in an attempt to raise agricultural production levels still higher.

Under N.E.P. heavy industry suffered, in comparison with agriculture and light industry, and did not attain the same levels of recovery:

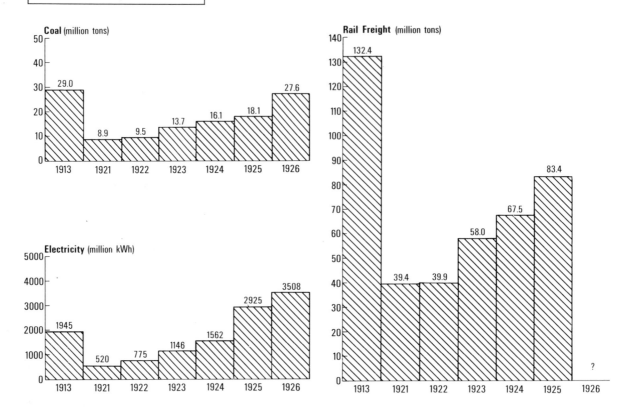

Production in the heavy industries 1913–26

Coal (million tons)

- 1913: 29.0
- 1921: 8.9
- 1922: 9.5
- 1923: 13.7
- 1924: 16.1
- 1925: 18.1
- 1926: 27.6

Rail Freight (million tons)

- 1913: 132.4
- 1921: 39.4
- 1922: 39.9
- 1923: 58.0
- 1924: 67.5
- 1925: 83.4
- 1926: ?

Electricity (million kWh)

- 1913: 1945
- 1921: 520
- 1922: 775
- 1923: 1146
- 1924: 1562
- 1925: 2925
- 1926: 3508

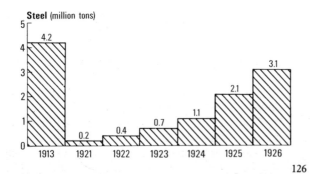

Steel (million tons)

- 1913: 4.2
- 1921: 0.2
- 1922: 0.4
- 1923: 0.7
- 1924: 1.1
- 1925: 2.1
- 1926: 3.1

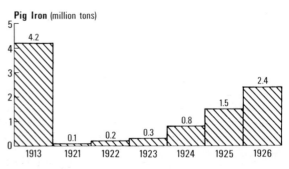

Pig Iron (million tons)

- 1913: 4.2
- 1921: 0.1
- 1922: 0.2
- 1923: 0.3
- 1924: 0.8
- 1925: 1.5
- 1926: 2.4

Although wage levels improved they did not attain 1913 standards, and N.E.P. brought with it an increase in unemployment. By 1924 the figure had reached 1¼ million and, at its height, was to approach 2 million.

N.E.P. lasted until 1928 when it was replaced by the First Five Year Plan and Stalin's offensive against the *kulaks*.

Assignment

1 a) What evidence is there of continuing peasant hostility to the Soviet government?
b) Why were many workers becoming discontented with the Communist Party?
2 What measures were taken under N.E.P. to stimulate
a) Agriculture   b) Industry   c) Trade
3 a) How successfull was N.E.P. in restoring agricultural output? Make use of the statistics provided.
4 a) Which sector of heavy industry experienced the greatest improvement in output during the N.E.P. period?
b) Suggest reasons why the output of the rest of heavy industry remained low.
5 What were N.E.P. men?

The Death of Lenin

In the summer of 1918 Lenin had been the victim of an assassination attempt. He recovered from the wounds he received from Kaplan's gun, but his health gradually deteriorated from this point on. He suffered two strokes in 1922 and, after a third

Lenin delivers a speech in Red Square, Moscow, on the first anniversary of the Bolshevik Revolution.

Lenin lies in state, Moscow 1924. The banner exhorts the people to greater 'unity, endurance and iron discipline'.

early in 1923, he lost the power of speech. He never fully recovered from this last stroke and died in January 1924 at the age of fifty-three. The Party turned his funeral into an elaborate ritual and Petrograd was renamed in his honour. His embalmed remains were entombed in Moscow's Red Square. It is unlikely that Lenin himself would have approved of the cult of Lenin which developed after his death, for he was a man who had preserved a taste for simplicity throughout his life. He bequeathed to the world the Leninist Party. He had shown that a small group of dedicated revolutionaries could seize power in a major state and then use the power of that state to ruthlessly destroy their rivals. It was an example which many revolutionary leaders attempted to follow in the succeeding years.

The Struggle for Leadership

As Lenin had not been able to play a full part in the work of government from 1922 onwards a struggle developed, between Leon Trotsky and Joseph Stalin, for the leadership of the Communist Party.

Trotsky Trotsky was the hero of the October Revolution and of the Civil War. He was widely regarded as a brilliant speaker, writer and thinker, although some found him ruthless, vain and lacking in charm. The writer and revolutionary, Victor Serge, wrote of him in 1921:

'No one ever wore a great destiny with more style. He was forty-one and at the apex of power, popularity and fame – leader of the Petrograd

128

Trotsky: the hero of the Revolution, 1923.

Trotsky put forward a theory of 'permanent revolution' in which the workers throughout the world were to be encouraged to stage their own revolutions and to set up socialist states, in the same way as the Russians had done. He believed, as did Lenin, that the new Soviet government could not survive alone in a world full of hostile capitalist states.

Lenin had appeared to regard Trotsky as his second-in-command throughout the Civil War period but not without reservations. In late 1922 he had written in his political testament:

> 'Comrade Trotsky is distinguished not only by his exceptional abilities – personally he is the most able man in the present central committee – but also by his too far reaching self confidence and a disposition to be too much attracted to the purely administrative side of affairs.'

Stalin Stalin had been born in Tiflis in Georgia in 1879 and christened Joseph Vissarionovich Dzhugashvili. His parents were of peasant stock and this was to make Stalin almost unique among the leading Bolsheviks. The young Dzhugashvili was sent to the seminary at Tiflis to study for the priesthood, but was expelled for the possession of revolutionary literature. He later wrote:

> 'I became a Marxist because of my social position (my father was a worker in a shoe factory and my mother was also a working woman) but also because of the harsh intolerance and Jesuitical discipline that crushed me so mercilessly at the Seminary. . . . The atmosphere in which I lived was saturated with hatred against Tsarist oppression.'

From 1901 onwards he was active as a revolutionary organizer for the Social Democratic Party among the oil workers of the Batum area, spreading

masses in two revolutions; creator of the Red Army which he had literally conjured out of nothing; personally the victor of several decisive battles . . . the acknowledged organizer of victory in the Civil War. . . .

His attitude was less homely than Lenin's with something authoritarian about it. . . . We had much admiration for him but no real love. His sternness, his insistence on punctuality in work and battle, the inflexible correctness of his demeanour in a period of general slackness all imparted a certain malice to the attacks that were made against him.'

129

Stalin's photograph in the police records.

propaganda and encouraging strikes. By 1905 Koba, as he was then known, was elected to the Baku Social Democratic Committee. Later, Stalin was to regard this as the formative period of his life.

In time he was arrested spending periods of imprisonment in both Baku and Batum before being exiled to Siberia in 1911. The following year he was elevated to the Bolshevik Central Committee, but his political influence was limited as he spent most of the succeeding five years in Siberian exile. Unlike most leading Bolsheviks he was not obliged to spend long years of exile outwith Russia and, as such, he remained a background figure, only emerging in March 1917 to assume the leadership of the Bolsheviks in revolutionary Petrograd. On Lenin's return Stalin loyally supported the *April Theses* and later, the decision to seize power in November.

He was rewarded for his loyalty, by Lenin in 1917, with the appointment of Commissar for Nationalities in the new Soviet Government. During the Civil War he played a prominent part in the defence of the city of Tsaritsyn, which was later to be known as Stalingrad.

Stalin's Rise to Power In 1919 Stalin had become Commissar of the Workers' and Peasants' Inspectorate, whose function was to eliminate abuses by the civil service. He had also by this time become a member of the Politbureau (the Party's inner group) and was in charge of the Control Commission which enquired into complaints against Party members. Through his command of this organization Stalin was able to begin the process of removing likely opponents from within the Party. The appointment which was to make Stalin a contender for supreme power came in 1922 when he became General Secretary of the Communist Party. The Secretariat appointed Party officials throughout the country and gave them their instructions. This enabled Stalin to place his own followers in key positions within the Party.

Lenin, although ill and nearing death, had seen the dangers which lay in Stalin's increasing power, and tried to influence events after his death by warning the Central Committee through his Testament:

> 'Comrade Stalin, having become General Secretary, has concentrated an enormous power in his hands, and I am not sure that he always knows how to use that power with sufficient caution...'

Stalin was to further infuriate Lenin by his inconsiderate treatment of his wife Krupskaya which resulted in an addition to the Testament.

Lenin in 1922: with his wife Krupskaya (left) and with Stalin (right)

'Stalin is too rude and this fault is insupportable in the office of General Secretary. Therefore I propose to the comrades to find a way to remove Stalin from that position and appoint to it another man who in all respects differs from Stalin only in superiority – namely more patient, more loyal, more polite, more attentive to comrades, less capricious etc.'

Stalin's Road to Dictatorship Stalin, aware of Lenin's anger, made great efforts not to antagonize his closest colleagues, with the result that when Lenin's testament became known Zinoviev and Kamenev agreed with Stalin that it should be suppressed, as they feared it would present Trotsky with an opportunity to make himself into a dictator. Stalin therefore retained his position as General Secretary and assumed power in a committee of three made up of himself, Kamenev and Zinoviev.

He then turned on Trotsky arguing against his 'permanent revolution' the theory of 'Socialism in one country': the Communists should concentrate on building up the Socialist State inside Russia itself before trying to export revolution to the rest of the world.

Trotsky, who lacked the temperament for intrigue and political infighting, was easily outmanoevred and gradually eased out of positions of power. In 1925 he was dismissed as War Commissar and removed from the Politbureau in 1926. In 1927 he was expelled from the Communist Party and in, 1929, exiled from Russia itself to eventually die in Mexico in 1940, by an ice-pick wielded by one of Stalin's agents.

In mid-1925 Stalin broke with Zinoviev and Kamenev who then attempted to ally themselves (too late) with Trotsky. In 1926 they too were driven from the Politbureau, and expelled from the

Trotsky in 1924. His decline from power had begun.

his erstwhile allies on the Right of the Party: Bukharin, the editor of *Pravda* and the Secretary of the Third International (Comintern); Tomsky, the trade union leader; Rykov the chairman of the Council of People's Commissars. The policy in question concerned the rapid industrialization of the country by the Five Year Plan and the proposed collectivization of the peasants. By 1930 all three had been driven from the Politbureau and demoted within the Party. By 1937 all three were dead.

By 1930 all serious political opposition to Stalin had been removed and the Politbureau was dominated by henchmen such as Molotov and Voroshilov. Stalin was now the unchallenged leader of the Soviet State.

Assignment

1 What do you think was the significance of Lenin's early death?
2 a) What do you understand by 'the theory of permanent revolution?
  b) Why do you think many people were suspicious of Trotsky?
3 a) Outline Stalin's career up to 1922
  b) What evidence can you put forward to show Lenin's dislike of Stalin?
4 By what means did Stalin make himself undisputed ruler of Russia?

Party in the following year. Both were to die after public trials in 1936.

Having dealt with the Left opposition of Trotsky, Zinoviev and Kamenev, Stalin now turned on

Questions

With the exception of questions 4 and 5 in Section 2, the following questions are taken from Scottish Certificate of Education past examination papers

Section 1 (from Paper I and Paper II Section B)

1 The following is an extract from an article in 'Iskra' written by Lenin shortly before the 1905 Revolution. In it he gives advice to fellow Bolsheviks.
'Organise for the determined struggle against autocratic government and against the whole of capitalist society. . . . We must train people who shall devote to the revolution not only their spare evenings, but the whole of their lives. . . . If we have a strongly organized party, a rebellion in a single locality may flare up into a victorious revolution.'
   a) Do you think that Lenin was justified in describing the government of Tsar Nicholas II as 'autocratic'? Give reasons.   5
   b) What did Lenin mean by 'capitalist society'?   4
   c) 'a victorious revolution'
      i) What do you think Lenin meant by 'a victorious revolution'?   2
      ii) Why do you think that in 1905 'rebellion' did not 'flare up into a victorious revolution'?   5
   d) How did the Bolsheviks organize themselves within Russia in response to Lenin's advice?   4
                                                                            (20)

2 The following two extracts relate to events concerning Bloody Sunday, January 9th (22nd) 1905.
   i) Petition of Workers and Residents of St. Petersburg for submission to Nicholas II.
   'We, workers and residents of the city of St. Petersburg, of various ranks and stations, our wives, children and helpless old parents, have come to Thee, Sire, to seek justice and protection . . . Our endurance is at an end; we have reached that awful moment when death is preferable to the continuation of intolerable suffering.'
   ii) Gapon's letter to the Tsar after Bloody Sunday.
   'The innocent blood of workers, their wives and children lies forever between thee, O soul destroyer, and the Russian people. Moral connection between thee and them may never more be . . . Let all the blood which has to be shed, hangman, fall upon thee and thy kindred.'

   a) How were the conditions for the workers so bad that 'death is preferable to the continuation of intolerable suffering'?   4
   b) Why was it to the Tsar that they went 'to seek justice and protection'?   3
   c) Is there any evidence in the first passage to show that the procession was intended to be peaceful?   3
   d) Illustrate from the two passages how Gapon's attitude to the Tsar changed, and explain why this change of attitude had taken place.   7
   e) Which sentence in the second passage proved to be prophetic, and why?   3
                                                                            (20)

3 In September, 1915, Tsar Nicholas took personal command of the Russian army. The following are two pieces of advice he received before he decided to take over.

I. From Rodzianko, the Chairman of the Duma.

'... at such a time, Your Majesty, you decide to remove the supreme commander, whom the Russian people still trusts absolutely. The people must interpret your move as one inspired by the Germans around you. ... Your Majesty's decision will appear to be a confession of the hopelessness of the situation.'

II. From Alexandra, the Tsar's wife.

'It is all much deeper than appears to the eye. ... You showing your mastery, proving yourself the autocrat without which Russia cannot exist. Being firm is your only saving. ... It will be a glorious page in your reign and Russian history, the story of these weeks and days.'

a) According to the evidence who advised the Tsar not to take command of the army? *1*

b) Give in your own words **one** of the arguments used in the passages
   i) in favour of the Tsar taking over command;
   ii) against the Tsar taking command. *4*

c) To whom is Rodzianko referring when he writes about 'the Germans around you'? *1*

d) i) Outline what had happened to the Russian armies in the first year of the war. *4*
   ii) Was the situation in September 1915 hopeless? Give reasons for your answer. *3*

e) Explain whether you think the Tsar's decision turned out to be 'a glorious page in your reign'. *4*

f) What does the Tsar's decision to take personal command of the Russian army tell you about his character? *3*

(20)

4 The following is an extract from the Tsar of Russia's 'Proclamation of Abdication', signed at Pskov, 2nd March, 1917.

'The internal disturbances which have begun among the people threaten to have a calamitous effect on the further conduct of a hard-fought war. The destiny of Russia, the honour of our heroic army, the welfare of the people ... demand that the war be carried to a victorious conclusion. ... The hour is already close at hand when our valiant army, together with our glorious allies, will be able to overwhelm the foe completely. In these decisive days ... we have deemed it our duty to help our people to draw close together ... and in agreement with the State Duma, we have judged it right to abdicate the throne of the Russian State.'

a) i) Explain the 'internal disturbances' to which the Tsar was referring. *6*
   ii) Why did he state that these disturbances would threaten to 'have a calamitous effect' on the war? *3*

b) Why did the Tsar think it necessary to abdicate at this time? *3*

c) 'to overwhelm the foe completely'. What chance did Russia have of doing this in 1917? *3*

d) i) What was the State Duma? *2*
   ii) Why did it agree that the Tsar should abdicate? *3*

(20)

5 The first extract below is from a report by Kuhlmann, the German Foreign Secretary, written in September, 1917. The second extract is from a Russian Army Intelligence report written in October, 1917.

I. 'Military operations on the Eastern Front were backed-up by intensive undermining activities inside Russia. . . . The Bolshevik movement could never have attained the scale or the influence which it has today without our continual support.'

II 'The Bolshevik wave is growing steadily owing to general disintegration in the rear, the absence of strong power, and the lack of supplies and equipment. . . . The dominant theme of conversation is peace at any price.'

a) i) How do the extracts differ in their explanation of the growth of support for the Bolsheviks in Russia in 1917?   4

ii) What other reasons can you suggest for this growth of support for the Bolsheviks?   3

b) 'The influence which it has today.'
How did the Bolshevik movement become one of influence in Russia before the October Revolution?   3

c) 'Intensive undermining activities inside Russia.'
i) Describe the event which in 1917 most clearly showed the German government's intention to help the Bolsheviks.   3

ii) Explain fully what you think the Germans hoped to achieve from their intensive undermining activities inside Russia.   3

d) 'Peace at any price.'
Why did many Russians want peace at any price in October, 1917?   4
(20)

6 Read the following passage, and then answer the questions following:
'The Russian Revolutions of 1917 were the culmination of a struggle of the mass of the Russian people to secure redress for their accumulated grievances. In 1905 the hardships of the war with Japan touched off a powerful revolutionary explosion that forced the Tsar to make significant concessions but he reduced them as soon as order had been restored. The Duma, which first met in 1906, achieved little in the way of basic reform. Thus the Russian Empire entered the First World War with its fundamental problems unsolved. The terrible calamities of the war intensified the impact of these problems and caused the fall of the Tsar.
There were two distinct revolutions in 1917. The first, the March Revolution, was a spontaneous, moderate affair which sought chiefly to replace the incompetent government of the Tsar with a more effective one of progressive political leaders. The November Revolution was very different; it was a far reaching social revolution organised and led by the Bolsheviks.'

Marks

a) '. . . to secure redress for their accumulated grievances.'
At the beginning of the twentieth century, what were the main grievances of:
i) the peasants;
ii) the industrial workers?   6

b) '. . . the hardships of the war with Japan'.
i) Why had Russia gone to war with Japan?   3

ii) Why did Russia lose the war and what effect did this have in Russia itself?   4

c) '. . . forced the Tsar to make significant concessions'.
i) What were the main concessions which the Tsar made?   3

ii) Why did the Duma achieve 'little in the way of basic reform'? 3

d) i) What were 'the terrible calamities of the war' referred to in the passage? 4

   ii) Why did these help to bring about the fall of the Tsar? 2

e) 'The first, the March Revolution, was a spontaneous, moderate affair'.

   i) Explain what is meant by 'spontaneous' and 'moderate' when referring to the March Revolution. 3

   ii) What were the main problems facing the new government after the March Revolution? 4

   iii) Why did it fall from power in November 1917? 4

f) In what ways was the November revolution 'a far reaching social revolution'? 4

(40)

7 Read the following passage, and then answer the questions following:

'The death of Lenin, early in 1924, marked the end of the most momentous six years in Russian history.

The Bolshevik seizure of power in 1917 had seemed most unlikely to be permanent, so great were the problems faced by the new government at home and abroad. Having accepted humiliating terms at Brest-Litovsk from the Germans in 1918, Lenin had soon found that several other foreign powers were unwilling to leave the Russians to settle their own affairs. Foreign help for the Whites had been insufficient, however, to deny the Red Army eventual triumph in the Civil War.

Meanwhile, events at the Kronstadt naval base in March, 1921, had convinced Lenin that War Communism could not solve the economic problems of Russia, and he had replaced it with a New Economic Policy which

ultimately ensured the survival of the régime. But the survival of that Bolshevik régime had been in no small part due to the qualities of character of Lenin, the man who had established it in 1917.'

Marks

a) Describe how 'the Bolshevik seizure of power' had been carried out in 1917. 5

b) 'humiliating terms at Brest-Litovsk . . .'

   i) Why did Lenin agree to the Treaty of Brest-Litovsk? 2

   ii) Why are the terms described as 'humiliating'? 4

c) 'Foreign help for the Whites.'

   i) What were the aims of the Whites? 3

   ii) Why and how did 'foreign powers' help them? 4

d) How do you account for the triumph of the Red Army in the Civil War? 5

e) 'events at the Kronstadt naval base.'

   i) Describe the events at the Kronstadt naval base in March, 1921. 3

   ii) How was the situation there dealt with by Lenin? 2

f) i) Why did 'War Communism' not solve the economic problems of Russia? 3

   ii) What were the main features of the New Economic Policy which replaced it? 5

g) What do you believe to have been the 'qualities of character' of Lenin which contributed to the survival of the Bolshevik régime? 4

(40)

Section 2 (from Paper II, Section C)

1 EITHER

A Imagine you were a Russian sailor who survived the Russo-Japanese War of

1904–1905. Describe your experiences during service with the fleet which sailed from the Baltic to the Far East, commenting on the state of the Russian navy, and the events you witnessed. *(20)*

OR

B Write eye-witness accounts of **two** of the following as if you were a person present when they took place:
   a) the events of Bloody Sunday, January, 1905;
   b) the assassination of Stolypin;
   c) the Kronstadt Naval rebellion. *(20)*

2 EITHER

A Imagine you are a War Correspondent given the task of covering the war on the Eastern Front in 1916. Write an article for your newspaper dealing with the following aspects – the state of the troops; adequacy of supplies, ammunition, medicine and food; leadership of the generals and officers; desertions and political agitators. *(20)*

OR

B Choose **two** of the following and write about them as if you were a person living during the period 1904–1924:
   a) The return of Lenin to Petrograd in April, 1917;
   b) the discovery of Rasputin's body in the River Neva;
   c) the last days of the Tsar and his family at Ekaterinburg. *(20)*

3 EITHER

A Imagine you are a Russian who is returning to Russia in 1922 after an absence of ten years. Write a letter to a friend in which you describe the changes you notice. You might refer to the government, the economy, religion and the daily life of the people. In the letter indicate whether you approve of the changes or not. *(20)*

OR

B Choose **two** of the following and write them as though you were the person living at the time:
   i) a soldier in General Kornilov's army defending the attempt to seize power;
   ii) a White Russian condemning the Treaty of Brest-Litovsk;
   iii) a supporter of Stalin campaigning for him to succeed Lenin.

4 Imagine you are a visitor to Russia in 1900. Write a letter home to your family giving your impression of village life as you have observed it on your travels.

5 Imagine you are a newspaper reporter assigned to Petrograd in the autumn of 1917. Write a report for your paper describing the immediate background to the Bolshevik uprising and the events of 6–7 November including the taking of the Winter Palace.

Index

Acknowledgements

The Publisher would like to thank the following for permission to reproduce photographs:

BBC Hulton Picture Library, pp. 6, 9 (left and right), 16, 22 (top), 23 (bottom), 24, 26 (centre), 34 (left), 39 (right), 43, 45 (right and left), 51 (top right and bottom), 52, 54 (right), 55, 60 (bottom), 61 (top), 65 (top right), 79 (bottom), 81, 84 (bottom), 85 (right), 91, 92 (left), 118, 119 (right), 129 and 132; Edimedia, pp. 22 (bottom), 36, 46 (right), 50, 68, 72, 77, 79 (top), 92 (right), 94, 95 (right), 98 (top), 106 and 116; Prince George Galitzine, p. 12; George Gibbes Collection, p. 101; GBUSSR Association, p. 17; Imperial War Museum, pp. 69, 104 (right) and 111 (top); Robert Hunt Library, pp. 32, 53 and 111 (bottom right); David King Collection, pp. 40, 109, 114, 115 and 130; Mansell Collection, pp. 35, 38 (bottom), 61 (left and right), 78 (top), 86 (bottom), 98 (bottom), 102, 104 (left), 107, 120 and 131 (left); Musée de l'Homme, p. 8; New York Public Library, pp. 41 and 63; Novosti, pp. 11 (right), 13 (top and bottom), 15, 19 (top and bottom), 21, 25, 34 (right), 42, 44 (right), 46 (left), 58, 64, 65 (top left), 66, 71, 74 (top and bottom), 93 (left), 95 (left), 99 (top), 111 (bottom left), 119 (left), 121 and 124; Popperfoto, pp. 7 (all), 31, 51 (top left), 54 (left), 65 (bottom), 67, 86 (top), 89, 99 (bottom) and 113; Roger-Viollet, p. 76; SCRUSSR, pp. 26 (top, bottom left, bottom centre and bottom right), 78 (bottom), 83, 85 (left), 93 (right), 96, 127 and 128; Ullstein, pp. 23 (top), 28, 29, 38 (top), 39 (left), 44 (left), 60 (top), 84 (top), 88 and 131 (right); UPI International, p. 122; Victoria and Albert Museum, p. 14; Mrs E. Zinovieff, p. 11 (left).

We would also like to thank Gwyneth Learner, of the GBUSSR Association, and George Gibbes, of St. Nicholas House, Oxford, for their help in our research. Picture Research by Ann Usborne.

Thanks are also due to the Scottish Examination Board for permission to print questions from past, History (Alternative), examination papers.

The Imperial Eagle represented on the front cover was made available by George Gibbes, of St. Nicholas House, Oxford, and was originally part of the Tsar's Royal Yacht.